HOL

Please return / renew by date shown.
You can renew it at:
norlink.norfolk.gov.uk
or by telephone: 0344 800 8006
Please have your library card & PIN ready

ılt

gs

iolving

oblems

NORFOLK LIBRARY
AND INFORMATION SERVICE

NORFOLK ITEM

30129 068 539 8

D1375224

Difficult
Dogs

An Everyday Guide to Solving
Behavioural Problems

Vanessa Stead

The Crowood Press

First published in 2011 by
The Crowood Press Ltd
Ramsbury, Marlborough
Wiltshire SN8 2HR

www.crowood.com

© Vanessa L. Stead 2011

636.7088

All rights reserved. No part of this publication may be reproduced
or transmitted in any form or by any means, electronic or
mechanical, including photocopy, recording, or any information
storage and retrieval system, without permission in writing from
the publishers.

British Library Cataloguing-in-Publication Data
A catalogue record for this book is available from the British
Library.

ISBN 978 1 84797254 5

Acknowledgements
I would firstly like to thank Mr and Mrs Player and their wonderful
dog Giles for being so obliging in taking so many of the training
shots invaluable for this book. I would like to thank all the staff
and dogs at the Dogs Trust Newbury for all their help and ongoing
support. Lastly I would like to thank my husband Sandrijn whose
support and assistance have been invaluable while making this
book; as well as helping rehabilitate the many lost canine souls
coming routinely through our house.

Typeset by Jean Cussons Typesetting, Diss, Norfolk
Printed and bound in China by Leo Paper Products Ltd

CONTENTS

INTRODUCTION

When your dog's behaviour becomes a problem, it can leave you feeling unhappy and unsure what to do, no matter how understanding and patient you may be. Problem behaviour can have significant implications for everybody concerned, both within and outside the home. In severe cases, when everyday life becomes seemingly impossible, you may even contemplate parting with your dog. This book aims to help you understand your dog's problematic traits, displays and actions, and show you how to decipher why they may have occurred. It explores problem behaviour in everyday life to show you that you can take control of it with dramatic impact. Each chapter uses real-life case studies and practical know-how to enable you to effectively change what is going wrong.

WHAT MAKES A PROBLEM DOG?

Quite simply, any dog can become a problem, usually when their behaviour has a disruptive and negative impact on everyday life. As a canine behaviourist I find particular problems crop up repeatedly: aggression, fear, attachment/security and general disobedience are four main reasons for concern. Stress entwines behavioural problems for both dog and owner and can't be underestimated. To understand how to change things, your first priority is to consider why these problems are occurring and where they

have come from. Determining the answer to this part of the puzzle allows you to tackle the cause of concern, which is absolutely critical. Without this knowledge it is easy to become trapped in a downward spiral and often make the issue worse through the use of incorrect treatment, usually punishment administered at the wrong time. This book aims to show you that your dog's behaviour is the result of changeable factors both internal and external. The interesting thing is that you can influence your dog on many levels, all of them connected, as the diagram opposite reveals.

UNDERSTANDING THE FACTORS THAT AFFECT BEHAVIOUR

The first section of the book begins by examining the link between health and behaviour, highlighting why you should always ensure your dog receives a clean bill of health before any training begins. Understanding how your dog learns and the factors that affect this process is vital to getting to the bottom of any problem and deciding how to change it. Your dog's environment, including the treatment he receives, is equally important. This is where the principle of dominance hierarchies and the use of different training methods come into play. These ideas are examined in detail in order to show that there is a far more effective way of changing behaviour than being aggres-

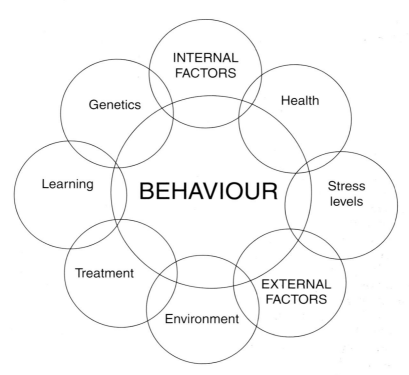

Behaviour is the result of a multitude of factors and is a variable system depending on internal and external components.

sive, confrontational and physically forceful. The book then explores the dramatic consequence for behaviour that can take place when the dog's environment doesn't cater for his maintenance behaviours and core needs. Finally, I examine the often underestimated effects of stress for you and your dog and highlight some everyday training and modification techniques that you can use to tackle these concerns successfully.

MAKING THE CHANGE

The second part of the book focuses on the next part of the process, one critical for all owners struggling with their dog's problems: shaping and changing behaviour.

We begin the process by examining what owners of rescue dogs struggle with on a daily basis: how to take control and manage and modify problem behaviour relating to dogs that have been through upheaval in their lives. Aggression and fear are major areas of concern for a huge number of owners; each needs a chapter to unravel the common problems associated with them. The next phase of the book takes you through an

ABOVE: Dogs are amazing animals, with individual personalities, likes and dislikes. This springer spaniel loves the water and is showing the inquisitive nature characteristic of man's best friend.

BELOW: These two dogs are enjoying a run outside, but you never know what's round the corner. This is why behavioural problems outside can be of great concern.

average day and shows how you can successfully address the common problems that occur in the home. However, behavioural problems are not limited to inside the home environment. When issues occur in the outside world they pose a whole new level of concern, mainly because it is a very difficult environment to control. This makes coping with problems, especially those posed by other people and other dogs, much more complicated and stressful, so I have developed a chapter to help you to tackle your dog's problems successfully when you leave the constraints of home.

The final section of the book tackles concerns relating to general obedience. Even wandering attention and lack of focus can become problems and make a difference to successfully tackling greater concerns. Effectively fine-tuning your dog's response to commands and improving his reactions can polish behaviour and restore harmony. The good news is that you can achieve this by positive reinforcement; training using kind, reward based methods will not only help your dog to learn desirable behaviour but can also develop the bond and relationship you have together. This book aims to show you how to manage and modify problem behaviour successfully by enabling you to see behaviour as a system.

Cohabitation with dogs can be rife with potential problems; the upside of this is that it can also be a wonderful relationship with friends, companions and bonds made for life. This book is dedicated to showing you how to repair the weak links in this relationship and build upon them by tackling the problems along the way. At each stage, kindness and thought are favoured over force and aggression, to help you build and shape behaviour rather than suppress it and break bonds.

1 HEALTH AND BEHAVIOUR

Before attempting any training or behavioural modification, it's vitally important to exclude any medical causes behind your dog's problematic displays.

A significant number of behavioural problems arise from health and pain issues, and if these aren't treated or taken into consideration you will miss a key part of the puzzle. Without this knowledge, you will definitely reduce your chances of successfully tackling the concern and possibly even risk increasing the severity of the problem.

Pain and the many conditions that cause it, hormonal imbalance, sensory dysfunction and sensory deterioration are four of the main health-related concerns that can lead to behavioural problems. Both here and later in the chapter I give you the same advice: take your dog to your vet for a full health check to exclude any medical concerns. This chapter will show you why this is so important and give you practical advice on how to help and support the behaviour of dogs suffering from health concerns.

PAIN

Quite understandably, pain can be a very common cause of problem behaviour. Pain is simply an unpleasant sensation that can range from acute (short term, such as somebody stepping on a dog's paw) through to chronic (long term, such as arthritis). Physiologically, pain often relates to potential and actual damage to the body's tissue, which commonly causes behaviour to change. Heartbeat, blood pressure, respiration and general activity can become dramatically different when pain strikes. Therefore it is essential that owners can identify what is normal behaviour for their dog as well as recognize changes, even subtle differences. Interestingly, the experience of a pain-provoking event can affect learning and cause the dog to be suspicious and react with fear/stress, avoidance and even aggression in the future. This highlights why every owner should look out for pain-related behaviours and be able to identify them, noticing any relevant changes in their dog's behaviour as an individual. It is important to remember that 'normal behaviour' varies from dog to dog; some dogs have higher pain thresholds than others and these thresholds can change as they mature and get older. You know your dog best, so if you see any signs of change, especially if they are presented repeatedly, seek veterinary help straight away. And try to note not only the behaviour being shown but also when and for how long it occurs. This will help you to judge your dog as an individual and if any of these signs are not in character, all may not be well. There are, however, standard signs of pain to look out for, together with the behavioural changes that accompany them.

Signs of pain-behaviour changes
The following are signs of pain that influence behaviour:

- Avoidance, including lifting limbs, and mouthing and pulling away when handled.
- Fear: freezing, staring, glaring, flight or fight mechanism including potential displacement behaviours such as fidgeting.
- Stress, producing panting, pacing, listlessness, facial ridges, displacement behaviours and repetitive or stereotypical actions.
- Irritability and potential for aggression both defensive and offensive, depending on the level of pain and past learning.
- Depression.
- Reduced mobility and muscle constriction; the dog may appear hunched up and stiff.

- Reluctance or excessive motivation to eat or drink.
- Vocalization such as whimpering, groaning, crying and yelping, usually high-pitched and especially when touched or handled.
- Increased attention to a particular area: licking, nibbling or biting, and repeatedly turning to look at a certain area of the body.

The Conditions that Cause Pain
A common cause of acute pain is injury, often caused by trauma such as impact, force and constriction (remember that the use of a choke chain covers all these three!). Anything that tears, pulls, stretches or actually damages the dog's tissue fibres can lead to pain anywhere in the body; organ failure and disease can also cause this response. Rubbing the same area of the body through repetitive movement such as pacing or through

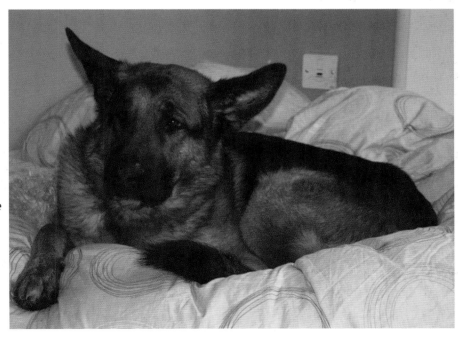

This dog is suffering from a severe stomach upset and painful sores. He's depressed and listless; his facial expression says it all.

Three different types of pain; three causes of a similar behavioural problem:			
CANINE CASE BEHAVIOUR	**PROBLEM BEHAVIOUR**	**PAIN**	**RESULT**
ZIGGY **Young** **(8 months)** **neutered** **Border** **Collie**	Defensive aggression towards dogs out on walks although has a history of living with and socializing successfully with various other dogs. Fast moving-high energy/impact individuals a particular concern. • Snapping • Biting • Lunging displayed	Acute foot pain; open wounds on pads through repetitive pacing in rescue kennel. The foot pain disabled Ziggy to a degree that caused him to be defensive because 1) He was unable to move rapidly to get away from any concern; 2) Active dogs put more pressure on him physiologically and psychologically.	With rest and care Ziggy's feet began to heal and his behaviour improved dramatically. As his feet improved he no longer felt and behaved in such a defensive manner when lively dogs approached him. The pain in this case definitely made a significant contribution to behaviour.
PICKLE **Mature** **(7 years)** **neutered** **male** **Terrier**	Aggressive behaviour towards owners upon waking/being woken up while sitting on the sofa. • Growling • Snapping • Biting displayed	Back pain diagnosed at the same time the aggressive behaviour started.	Back pain treated and behaviour modification focused on building Pickle's security; giving him his own space free from constant risk of being disturbed. This two-way plan helped Pickle to overcome his lack of security and the problem behaviour stopped.
TED **Adult** **(3 years)** **neutered** **male** **Labrador**	Defensive aggression towards dogs – particularly lively individuals that jump up at him. • Growling • Snarling • Snapping • Biting displayed	Double elbow dysplasia diagnosed at the same time behaviour occurred. Operation carried out to treat the concern and pain reduced however sign of arthritis developing (future pain possible)	Although Ted's condition improved and his pain reduced the learnt defensive association continued. He required further confidence/coping mechanism training to help him overcome the problem. It is important to remember that underlying pain may cause future concern and care must be taken to watch his signals carefully and protect where possible from lively, forceful play.

This lively pair are enjoying a rough play session. Some dogs can find this difficult to cope with if they are in pain.

poorly fitting equipment such as collars and harnesses of the wrong size are examples of mechanical force that can cause pain.

Extremes of temperature, chemicals, and electric shocks can also provoke pain, and acute pain can be caused by toothache, cuts, bruises and abrasions. This can result in the behaviour changes mentioned above, but it is also worth remembering that if your dog is suffering from any painful complaint, stress will be a very likely by-product.

I can't continue this chapter without briefly referring to examples of training implements that can cause acute pain.

LEFT: Three different painful conditions and their corresponding behaviour.

Although these methods are designed to be relatively short term and abrupt, through repeated use they can lead over time to long-term physiological and behavioural effects. Continued use of pain when the dog is unable to escape and avoid it can lead to a state called 'conditioned suppression', where a dog's behaviour ceases and he shuts down altogether. Some may think that this means that the treatment has worked; however, far from dealing with the cause of the problem such methods merely suppress the true behaviour and can have dramatic and detrimental impacts for the dog's future mental state. The simple message is: don't use choke chains, electric shock collars and prong collars, and remember that using painful methods (even yanking or pulling the dog on a flat

13

collar) can be hugely detrimental to your dog's overall behaviour.

Chronic Pain

If a painful condition continues and even exceeds the 'normal' healing time for the condition, it can become chronic, which has additional implications for both behaviour and welfare. Conditions that cause chronic pain in dogs include: hip dysplasia, arthritis, organ disease or failure, cancer and back/limb problems. When pain continues to plague the dog the signs are likely to become increasingly severe. If any of the dog's maintenance behaviours (eating, drinking, sleeping, urination and defecation) are affected, this is very likely to result in behavioural consequences. Chronic pain can cause a dramatic increase in irritability and disturbance to sleep. Some dogs may even struggle to reach the deeper sleep stages where rest and repair take place. If you do have a dog suffering from a concern related to chronic pain and under veterinary supervision, there are ways to help it both in and out of the home.

- Always ensure that you cater for the basics and give priority to your dog's maintenance needs. If he is a little stiff or immobile, ensure that food and water stations are within easy reach (maybe even raised on a stand). And be sure to help these dogs go to the toilet area regularly; don't wait for them to struggle to hold themselves in. Remember that if they are suffering from a painful condition it may take them longer to get to this area and helping them to do this can really make things easier.
- Protect them: it's even more important to ensure that dogs suffering from

painful conditions have a quiet, restful place in the home that is warm, safe and secure and away from comings and goings. This will enable them to rest away from the hustle and bustle of family life and provide valuable respite from children and other pets. Dogs in pain can be more sensitive to movement and become particularly concerned, even defensive, if threatened. So take care to allow space when walking past them and avoid walking over the top of them. Limit play and particularly keep watch over youngsters interacting and playing with your dog as they may be more inclined to instigate rough games – absolutely not advisable with a dog suffering from long-term pain.

- Keep watch when out and about. On walks, judge interaction with other dogs carefully. If your dog starts to show concern, keep moving and encourage him to distance himself. Another dog instigating a rough or over-zealous game could worry your dog, who may already be more sensitive to interactions and potentially defensive or aggressive.
- Look, listen and learn. Watch out for any sign that your dog is experiencing pain or feeling threatened by a stimulus from inside or outside the house. This may be the first indication that something isn't right, perhaps telling you to stop what you're doing or that something needs changing. Freezing, staring, glaring, growling and showing teeth are all signals that your dog may be experiencing pain during an interaction. Activities such as grooming, fitting equipment, bathing and general handling are potential risk areas, and it's advisable to take notice of any signals, however slight, that

This terrier is having his paw checked as he appears in pain. Take care to handle situations like this carefully.

indicate that your dog is not confident about the situation.

THE ENDOCRINE SYSTEM

Hormones have a vital part to play throughout a dog's life. They are chemicals produced in the body and released to influence cells, organs, body function, physiology and psychology. Hormonal changes and influences can have dramatic effects on behaviour, emotions and mood. They are responsible for many physiological processes from development (for example, regulating growth and sexual development) to processing food and blood sugar levels (metabolism) and regulating the energy system in times of threat and conflict through the stress response (the flight or fight reaction). Hormone production and release occurs in particular glands (including the pituitary, thyroid and adrenal glands) as well as in organs such as the testes, ovaries, kidneys and liver, which have other functions besides hormone production. As hormones are responsible for such a large part of the body's function and process, any imbalance can have major effects on health and behaviour. Similarly, disruptions to the natural hormonal system such as spaying and neutering can cause changes in behaviour.

Endocrine System

Endocrine disease can relate to over-production (hyper secretion) or under-production (hypo secretion) of hormone levels; both can unbalance the system. Therefore anything that changes the 'normal' hormone quantities can have effects. Damage, deterioration and the effects of tumours can cause major disruption to hormone secretion. The following endocrine diseases can affect your dog's health and behaviour:

- Diabetes mellitus. In Type I there is insufficient production of insulin in specialized cells in the pancreas, possibly through damage to these cells; this prevents the metabolism of sugar and interferes with energy production. Type II diabetes, when insulin is produced but can't be used effectively, is much rarer in dogs. Symptoms can include increased thirst, frequent urination and increased hunger, weight loss (despite eating), rapid onset of blindness and general lack of energy.
- Addison's disease (hypoadrenocorticism) is a deficiency of glucocorticoids and mineralocorticoids, the main hormones cortisol and aldosterone from the adrenal glands. It can create symptoms of increased thirst, lack of energy, weight loss and weakness, depression and mood changes, diarrhoea and dehydration, as well as critical signs of low body temperature, shaking, collapse and low heart rate. Particular times of concern are stressful situations, due to the imbalance of a principal stress hormone, cortisol.
- Cushing's disease (hyperadrenocorticism) is over-production of adrenal gland hormones such as cortisone, and is often related to tumours, usually linked to the pituitary gland and causing growth of the adrenal glands and increased hormonal production. Tumours in the adrenal glands can also cause concern. Sufferers often show increased motivation to eat and drink, and increased urination. They may also have a pot-bellied appearance and suffer from hair loss, lethargy and weakness.
- Hypothyroidism is deficient production of thyroxin, which is responsible for metabolic function, and it slows the energy process. Causes can relate to inflammation, degeneration, or tumours located in the thyroid or pituitary glands. Hypothyroidism can cause weight gain (without the appetite growing), general decreased interest in daily life and activities such as play, exercise and training, irritability and aggression, more frequent/longer bouts of sleeping and rest, increased suffering or concern in the cold, and stomach problems such as constipation and diarrhoea.
- Hyperthyroidism is increased production of thyroxin in the thyroid glands, which increases metabolic function. Potential causes are tumours of the thyroid glands. This condition is much rarer in dogs than hypothyroidism. Symptoms include increased appetite, weight loss (though eating the same amount), excessive thirst, diarrhoea, and frequent and increased urination.

OPPOSITE: *The principal areas of sensory dysfunction to be aware of, and what to do to help.*

SENSORY DYSFUNCTION	IMPACT AND PROBLEMS	WHAT TO DO
Sight	• Sight impairment can cause dogs to become wary of people and other animals through inability to process what they are seeing: can cause defensive/aggressive displays as figures may appear threatening through inability to see clearly. • Sight loss can cause dogs to become defensive and nervous in new situations and worried about approaching people/ other animals especially if they are forceful/playful. • Reduced vision may also disrupt the dog's ability to judge signals and can easily misread situations.	• Take care when introducing people; organize interactions calmly, allowing your dog to approach and investigate; avoid visitor leaning over and frightening them. • If possible ask the visitor to sit down in the home for your dog to investigate without height adding to their concern (keep objects in the same place to build security and reduce stress). • Allow warning, use vocals and gentle touch (from side/ front) when approaching rather than abruptly interacting/waking the dog. Remember if visuals are decreased ensure you remember to engage the dog's other senses. • While out walking watch for signs of concern; any freezing; tension building and ensure your dog knows where you are. Keep relatively close by wherever possible and be ready to call to them to move on if concern strikes.
Hearing	• Even a slight loss of hearing can create problems for dogs that as a species ordinarily have acute hearing ability. • Jumpiness, agitation and nervousness can accompany these individuals. • Interactions with people and other animals can easily become frightening. • Deaf dogs (either from birth or later onset) can be unaware of auditory commands or warning signals from other dogs. This can make daily life and interaction difficult and potentially hazardous.	• Supervise interactions with others (particularly young children and other dogs). Ensure they give the dog plenty of warning as stated above remembering that it's advisable to move into the dog's field of view before interacting. • Teaching sign language can be extremely useful in communicating to dogs with auditory concerns. Additionally teaching them to keep 'checking in' and watching you for instruction is useful in daily life and interactions.

Problem Behaviours Associated with Endocrine Disease

Dogs suffering from endocrine disease may show a number of presenting signs but their imbalanced internal state can have an adverse effect on their behaviour. Hormone deficiency can cause a general lack of interest in life, irritability and depression; increased hormone production can lead to hyperactivity, nervousness and even aggression (including sudden onset). Hormone imbalance can cause fatigue and muscle weakness, and cause your dog's behaviour to change. This can disrupt normal walks and play sessions and some dogs can even become agitated when introduced to new individuals. Others experience mood swings and a change in greeting behaviour. They may find times of stress particularly difficult to cope with and become easily concerned. Toileting accidents may occur much more frequently despite your dog being fully house-trained in the past. Veterinary intervention and care is needed in all cases but the following points will help you to manage problem behaviours often associated with these health concerns and support and encourage favourable behaviour.

- Be stress aware. Dogs suffering from hormonal imbalance can find stressful events very difficult to cope with. Try to keep things calm and relaxed and diffuse tension by keeping calm yourself and managing situations carefully. Trips to the vet and car journeys may be red zone areas; plan events in advance so that you are prepared and always ensure you have water available.
- Don't forget the maintenance behaviours: ensure that you cater for your dog's basic needs, which may be elevated due to hormonal influence.

Make certain that food and water stations are kept in the same place and that water is always available and topped up, and give your dog plenty of opportunities to go to the toilet, because increased elimination behaviour can cause toilet mishaps if not addressed. Just as dogs in pain suffer from increased lethargy and depression, hormonal imbalance can change the dog's metabolism, causing him to need higher levels of rest; give him plenty of time to rest and relax undisturbed.

- Maintain a balanced routine. Keeping your dog's routine simple to follow and the same every day can help to relieve stress and build his confidence and security. By stabilizing feeding and exercise opportunities you can successfully put balance into the imbalanced dog's life.
- Don't ask too much: keep things simple, including commands and training. Try to work at your dog's level and don't confuse them with complicated instructions. Perfecting the basic commands is a great starting place, and be sure to use lots of reward to support positive emotions. Remember, hormone imbalance can really affect how your dog is feeling, so anything that builds and supports security will be really beneficial.

SENSORY DYSFUNCTION AND DETERIORATION

Your dog's senses are very important in facilitating everyday behaviour. Sensory dysfunction affecting sight, smell, hearing, touch or taste can cause considerable behaviour problems and put pressure on the dog's ability to cope with 'normal' situations. Owners should be aware of

THE AGEING PROCESS: SENSORY LOSSES

As a dog ages, changes occur to the sensory system that feeds information into the dog's brain. Food may lose flavour, sounds become less easy to hear and sights become distorted and blurred. Dogs use their senses as part of their danger detection system; failure to detect threats can be very disturbing. Failing eyesight creates similar problems (cataracts are a common eye concern in older dogs). With age comes the loss of both types of retinal cell in the eyes, and lenses can lose their elasticity, causing blurring and difficulty in focusing. Misjudging spaces or walking into objects can be a sign that your dog's eyesight is deteriorating, as well as changes to the eye's physiology such as clouding, inflammation and redness.

In a youthful dog, the brain sends messages from cell to cell through connecting filaments. In the ageing dog, the filaments contract and lose some of their contacts with other cells. This means that information must pass through a different route and will be processed more slowly. Another problem is that, once stimulated, the cells remain programmed for abnormally long periods, preventing further information from being absorbed. This affects a dog's short-term memory, making dogs irritable when disturbed, slow to obey commands, and causing problems with orientation and learning. Previous daily activities may become ritualized; for example, some individuals may ask to be let out to urinate not because of need but because some cue has stimulated the cell linked to this action. The cell cannot evaluate the cue; it merely triggers imprinted actions. The dog may also return to his feed station as if he is hungry because the original cue remains and the cells cannot override the imprinted actions. Repeated behaviours and displacement actions can become common signs of cognitive deterioration. Cognitive Dysfunction Syndrome (CDS) can cause aggression and uncharacteristic behaviour due to brain degeneration. Symptoms of old age, sensory dysfunction, hormonal imbalance and general pain show significant similarities. This highlights once again why it is so important to ensure that your dog undergoes medical examination by your vet to get to the bottom of your concerns.

any changes to their dog's sensory abilities. The most common concerns relate to the dog's ability to see and hear.

SENSORY DETERIORATION IN ELDERLY DOGS

Sensory deterioration accompanies many dogs as they move through maturity into their senior years. The general definition of old age is the last third of the normal life expectancy for any particular breed. Larger breeds tend to age more rapidly than smaller dogs, so a St Bernard will be more mature at five years old than a miniature poodle of the same age. Elderly dogs can develop specific behaviour problems due to declining sensory abilities. These include 'grumpiness' and irritability, even outbursts of potential aggression, confusion, stress and anxiety.

Mainly because of physiological and sensory deterioration, dogs are less able to cope with stress as they age. I examined the implications of vision and hearing dysfunction in an earlier table and the same management rules apply. It's also important to reduce stress wherever possible and there are measures you can take to deal effectively with these problems.

Practising simple commands and tricks for praise and reward can be a great way to gently exercise your older dog.

Deterioration of the brain can be lessened by providing a stimulating environment, but ensure that you keep things simple. New toys and simple games can help to exercise the brain. We know that a reduction of oxygen to the brain results in impaired brain function, so encourage more oxygen to circulate by gentle exercise. Once again, monitor your dog's reaction to any games you play with him, and avoid them if he becomes frustrated or confused.

Deteriorating eyesight and hearing can make it more difficult for dogs to rest, so it is important that your dog can get out of his bed easily and that his weight is evenly distributed to reduce pressure on his joints. Make sure that his bed is in a warm, quiet, draught-free place where he will not be disturbed by people constantly walking past, or be pestered by children or other pets.

Sensory deterioration can cause elderly dogs to be slower in both recognizing the need to relieve themselves and in getting to the place where they can do it. Bear this in mind in your planning.

EPILEPSY

Besides the four health-related concerns that we examined in this chapter – pain, hormonal imbalance, sensory dysfunction and sensory deterioration – there are also neurological concerns. I come across behaviour cases on a daily basis that are fuelled by health concerns. Sudden-onset aggression where the dogs don't remember or recollect what they have done can be linked to neurological problems such as idiopathic epilepsy (epilepsy with no known cause). Thankfully these occur more rarely than other aggressive motivators but truly random incidents of unprovoked aggression are very serious and as such should be examined professionally. Medical and behavioural treatment can work fantastically well alongside each other to address the multitude of factors surrounding these concerns. The table overleaf reveals an insight into epilepsy and the problems it can cause as a major neurological concern.

HEALTH CONCERN	RESULTING BEHAVIOUR	BEHAVIOUR PLAN
NEUROLOGICAL • **Epilepsy** Characterized by seizures (often reoccurring) Causes: metabolic dysfunction, organ failure (reactive epilepsy) brain trauma, tumours (secondary epilepsy); idiopathic epilepsy has no known cause.	Aggressive behaviour can accompany epilepsy in dogs sometimes before, during and after episodes. Aggression can be sudden, seemingly unprovoked. In some cases the dog may return to display 'normal' behaviour rapidly without the appearance of remembering the event. Some dogs may even show: glazed eyes, confusion, 'stare into space' as seizures affect their mental ability	Truly unprovoked and random aggression through epileptic origin can be extremely concerning and veterinary attention and professional behavioural advice is needed as soon as possible. It is vital to seek professional help to decide the best course of action. Maintaining a calm and balanced daily routine is important. It is vital to be extremely vigilant to any signs of concern; potential aggression such as freezing, staring, glaring and stop what you are doing. A balanced diet is also vitally important.

One of the principal health issues that can cause behaviour to change and become problematic.

2 PROBLEM DOG, LEARNT BEHAVIOUR?

You probably began reading this book in order to try to unravel your dog's problem behaviour, because you need and want to change it. When a dog's behaviour is problematic, troubling sights and sounds, and upsetting feelings, make owners think back to how it came about. This seems very reasonable; if you can untangle how a problem behaviour has been learnt, you have gained an essential tool that will enable you to understand how things have gone wrong and, very importantly, how to put them right. In this chapter I will show you who the problem dogs really are, how they may have learnt to be this way, and the contribution made to this process by the dog's acute senses. Real case studies will help you to understand your dog's behaviour in a way you may never have been able to before.

WHO ARE THE PROBLEM DOGS?

Quite simply, any dog can be or become a problem to live with! This huge generalization is based on three main factors:

1. Many of the dog's natural behaviours and core needs can be incompatible with life with their owners. For example, dogs with very high energy levels

The little black and white dog (standing) is posturing in what could be seen as a threatening position to the dog underneath.

23

will be at odds living with a family who don't have time to give them any exercise.

2. Owners can miscommunicate with their dogs and misunderstand them. For example, behaviour perceived as dominant may actually be the result of other motivating factors such as fear. The misunderstanding of behaviour often leads to incorrect treatment, which usually makes the problem worse because the cause has not been taken into consideration!

3. Owners can use inappropriate and unnecessary training methods and treatment, such as pain, fear and punishment. For example, striking a dog for growling when approached while eating from his food bowl can teach the dog a negative association and insecurity around food resources in the future.

The good news for both our species is that dogs can and do make wonderful companions and have a natural affinity with human society. This affinity depends on several factors such as the dog's genetic disposition, development, environment, treatment and, of course, learning. Imbalance in any of these or disruption to them can create potential problems, but begin by considering that dogs are intelligent, intuitive animals that learn, remember and change depending on the experiences they go through internally and externally. Always try to remember that dogs interact with humans on an individual level; the best relationships require give and take on both sides. Rules are important in all relationships; however, it's critically important to enforce these in a way that does not disrupt trust, confidence and security. Trust, confidence and security are critical for a stable relationship; repeatedly in my work I see these key areas in jeopardy.

HOW DOGS LEARN BEHAVIOUR

As a dog owner you probably recognize that you can teach your dog specific behaviours and tasks. While teaching dogs, it is easy to forget how they actually learn to act on command: learning is inextricably linked to teaching, which is

Stable relationships require trust on both sides. Giles's slight head tilt and focused expression show him trying to work out what to do.

an invaluable tool for all behaviourists, trainers and owners, but especially for those needing to identify, manage and modify problem behaviour.

AN ENEMY TO LEARNING

Every living being has a set of core needs that must be met in order for them to survive. These needs include eating, drinking, sleeping, defecating and urination. If we or any other living animal were unable to meet any one of these needs we would not be able to survive. Additionally, if any core need is compromised it causes stress and stress is an enemy of learning. Problem behaviour can be a by-product of a dog unable to meet any one of their basic requirements. Take time to consider your own dog and the problems you are having; are his essential requirements catered for? The impact of disrupted needs on your dog will be discussed in more detail in Chapter 3; for now, however, it remains an important consideration.

CLASSICAL CONDITIONING

In the early nineteenth century a Russian scientist named Ivan Petrovich Pavlov was working with dogs when he noticed something he called 'psychic' salivation. Put simply, a dog would begin to salivate when any cue for feeding was presented to him – his food bowl, the person who normally fed him, or even the sound of that person's footsteps. He named this 'psychic' salivation because it occurred in the absence of food. He went on to examine this phenomenon in a series of experiments culminating in the discovery of a type of learning known as Classical Conditioning.

PICTURE THIS: A CLASSICAL CONDITIONING EXAMPLE

Jimmy the foxhound is always getting extremely dirty clambering through the undergrowth out on walks. His owners regularly wash him in the shower when they arrive back home. The shower is adjacent to the bathroom and whenever anybody flushes the handle of the lavatory the shower water becomes extremely hot. Over time, after several events of this kind, Jimmy started jumping out of the shower, alarmed and concerned, every time he heard the flush of the lavatory before the water had become hot. The unconditioned stimulus is Jimmy reacting to the hot water (this is an automatic reflex); the sound of the lavatory flush becomes the conditioned stimulus.

ASSOCIATIVE LEARNING

Operant Conditioning

When your dog learns through operant conditioning (also known as instrumental learning) their intended behaviour is met by a consequence. The nature of the consequence can influence the frequency of the behaviour and can even lead to it becoming more or less frequent. For example, using a positive consequence means adding something when the dog behaves in a certain way; using a negative consequence takes something away. Positive and negative consequences are closely related to the concepts of reinforcement and punishment, which can also be positive or negative. Examining these principles will help you to understand how your dog may have learnt to behave, desirably or indeed undesirably, and how to change this behaviour.

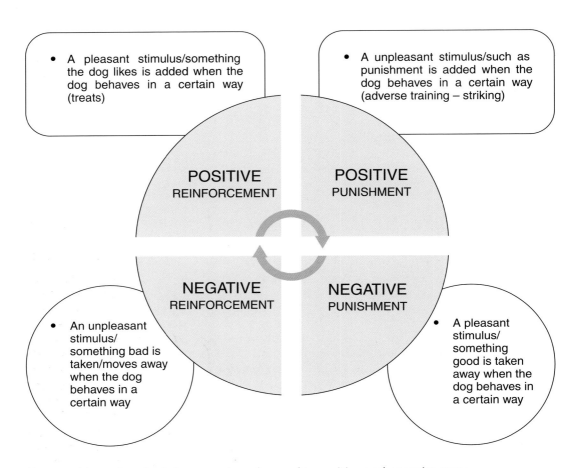

- A pleasant stimulus/something the dog likes is added when the dog behaves in a certain way (treats)

- A unpleasant stimulus/such as punishment is added when the dog behaves in a certain way (adverse training – striking)

POSITIVE
REINFORCEMENT

POSITIVE
PUNISHMENT

NEGATIVE
REINFORCEMENT

NEGATIVE
PUNISHMENT

- An unpleasant stimulus/ something bad is taken/moves away when the dog behaves in a certain way

- A pleasant stimulus/ something good is taken away when the dog behaves in a certain way

How punishment and reinforcement can be used in positive and negative ways.

PICTURE THIS: AN OPERANT CONDITIONING EXAMPLE

Tommy the springer spaniel loves swimming in the river. He enjoys it so much that he often does not want to come back when called. His owners have tried shouting at him to get his attention but this rarely seems to work. They then introduced a packet of tasty treats into the equation and whenever Tommy came when called he received a really tasty treat. Over time Tommy began to come back much more promptly because he began to realize that when he came back to his owners something pleasant happened (he received a treat). The treat is the positive reinforcement.

Using positive reinforcement during training (adding something pleasant when the dog offers a certain behaviour) is invaluable because it is an essential tool to promote feel-good emotions. This helps to produce a happy dog who is more co-operative, willing, able and wanting to learn – undoubtedly a much easier dog to work with and modify. Reward can vary from vocal praise to strokes, pats, toys, chews, clicker and treats. Punishment can undeniably suppress problem behaviour when it happens, but it doesn't tackle the underlying cause; this is the fundamental issue with using such punitive actions in behaviour modification. The case study of Charlie shows how this can happen.

Multiple Approaches, One Desired Outcome

Charlie is a year-old male labrador, bought as a ten-week-old puppy. He has recently begun to show aggressive displays while eating from his food bowl when his owners approach. His vet has excluded any medical concerns behind the behaviour but on further exploration an important discovery was made: Charlie was born in a large litter of puppies that had to compete for their food. When Charlie arrived home from the breeder he was underweight with suspected bite scars on his body. Charlie eats extremely rapidly and always appears hungry although he is in perfect condition, fed high-quality feed of the correct amount and is the correct weight for his breed and age.

The first methods his owners used to tackle the concern involved punishment: striking him (positive punishment), placing him on a lead and pulling him away from his bowl (positive and negative punishment), and taking his bowl away from him while he was eating (negative punishment). Although it may seem logical to do this to stop the behaviour from being displayed and teach the dog that this behaviour is unacceptable, bad or naughty, such actions may be counterproductive because of how the behaviour was learnt – the true reason behind these actions. Therefore effectively modifying his behaviour relies on our understanding of how Charlie had learnt to behave in this way and why.

As a puppy Charlie had to quite literally fight for his food. He was not able to receive enough when he was a young puppy (hence his low body weight), which taught him to value food very highly. Charlie had learnt through heavy competition and lack of food at a young age to eat as fast as he could to prevent someone else from getting it, and to guard and protect this resource which grew in value each time it was scarce. This pattern of learning set Charlie up for potential concern in his home when faced with events to trigger this learnt response. Charlie's owners unknowingly stimulated this learning through using punishment; the behaviour began to increase in severity every meal time, every day.

Once the punishment techniques began, Charlie became increasingly aggressive and sensitive to any people near his food bowl. This is because Charlie began to learn through classical and instrumental learning to protect this valuable resource more each day the treatment was applied. The more his food is taken from him, the higher in value it becomes; the more he is punished during feeding, the more insecure and threatening people become when close to his food. If we look at how Charlie had learnt to behave in this way we learn that

This dog is happily eating from her food bowl while this photograph is being taken.

THE DOG'S SENSES AND THEIR ROLE

The dog's sensory abilities have been fundamental in the evolution of the human–canine relationship over thousands of years. The dog's many valuable sensory genetic traits have facilitated a perfect match for humans as formidable team mates, providing hunters, herders, transporters and guarders throughout history. These senses have in part been harnessed through domestication and trained to serve us. Humans continue to use the dog's senses and natural behaviours to their advantage. Many owners don't have to train their dogs to bark when outsiders approach, irrespective of whether or not it is desirable. Other people, by contrast, go to great lengths to fine-tune the dog's senses. Examples of such dogs include sniffer dogs to detect illegal or dangerous substances, guide dogs to help people, and search and rescue dogs used all over the world to find lost and injured people. Although these senses were and are of great use to humans, today they can place the dog at odds with their owners. There is no doubt that dogs' differing sensory abilities predispose them to learn and behave in ways that owners may find problematic.

The Senses

Dogs and humans both have five senses: sight, smell, touch, taste and hearing. Humans prefer to rely on their vision and hearing senses in everyday life, although olfaction (smell) and taste are deeply ingrained in our evolution as part of the animal kingdom. For your dog, life is somewhat different; the senses that have made dogs successful as a species have become, in part, a major disadvantage. In the modern world, previously desirable

the root of the problem is Charlie's insecurity around food. Charlie values food extremely highly and has become increasingly anxious that someone will take it away; this produces a dog ready to fight for food, which is a natural response to the lessons he has learnt. I examine the specifics of this concern in Chapter 9. For now, however, I hope that this example helps you to see how important it is to consider the part learning has to play in problem behaviour.

LEARNED HELPLESSNESS

In early 1965, Martin E.P. Seligman and his colleagues were studying the relationship between fear and learning in dogs. Using classical conditioning techniques, Seligman paired a buzzer with an electric shock. The dog was restrained during the learning phase in the belief that after he had learnt to associate the buzzer with the shock, he would, if possible, run away on presentation of the buzzer.

To test this they put the conditioned dog into a box, which was divided into two compartments by a fence. The dog could easily jump over the fence, but to their amazement, when the buzzer sounded, the dog did nothing. Then they wondered what would happen if they gave him a shock, but again nothing happened. The dog just lay there. However, when they put a new dog into the box, that had never experienced the inescapable shock, it immediately jumped over the fence to the other side.

Seligman concluded that the conditioned dog had learnt that trying to escape from the shocks was futile. He had learnt to be helpless! This was the opposite of the predictions of the time, which argued that the dog would have needed to be given a reward (positive reinforcement) to stay where it was on hearing the buzzer, rather than leaping over the fence. Learned helplessness can also occur in dogs that are frequently punished. They can become so

This chocolate labrador is a very fearful dog and is showing concern at being in close proximity to the person sitting down.

confused that they give up, because they realize that nothing they can do will stop the punishment. Suppressing behaviour in this way is abnormal and can also be dangerous: dogs in a state of learned helplessness may suddenly respond aggressively to a frightening event in an all or nothing attempt to survive. Additionally, when a dog enters this state of mind no new behaviours will be offered; your dog no longer has the ability to perform a desirable behaviour and instead shuts down altogether – a terrible consequence for your dog and very worrying for future behaviour, which is likely to return and increase in severity.

In this photograph the same chocolate labrador is much more relaxed, confident and engaged, and therefore able to learn new behaviour much more easily.

This dog is displaying tracking behaviour, which can often cause dogs to become absorbed in scent and slow to obey commands.

abilities have now unfortunately become the root of many common problems. Understanding how dogs see, smell and hear the world differently from humans can help you to get to the bottom of problem behaviours that arise from these differences.

Sight

Put simply, dogs see the world differently to humans. The vision of dogs is similar to that of red/green colour-blind humans (deuteranopes) and their ability to focus on near objects is also not as good as a human's. Additionally they have a smaller binocular overlap (the section of a scene that can be seen by both eyes). Greater binocular overlap is important when focusing on objects close up, whereas the reverse is true when focusing at a greater distance, a trait very useful to hunters and the Canidae family in general.

The dog's visual abilities are also superior in relation to function in low light, field of view, ability to distinguish different shades of grey, and ability to detect motion. This is important because it enables us to understand how the dog sees the world and the behaviours he learns through his different visual abilities. It can also help you to understand why problem behaviours come about. Problems relating to a dog's sight abilities include:

- chasing prey;
- reactive, fearful or aggressive behaviour towards stimuli (at far distances as well as nearby);
- reaction to body language and movement (negative for the fearful dog who shudders at every movement and raise of the hand);
- loss of focus on owners in low light out on walks; at this time of night the dog's vision comes into its element and he can be extremely reactive to every movement in the bushes.

Smell

The dog's sense of smell is really quite incredible. They are used all around

SAME WALK, DIFFERENT TIME: DIFFERENT DOG

Jerry the German shepherd mix is an even-tempered family dog. He is taken for regular walks twice daily, in the morning and the early evening. During the summer months Jerry is relaxed and confident when walking past most strangers, although he has been known to bark at the occasional passer-by. As autumn turns to winter Jerry is taken on his second walk of the day in the dark. He begins to bark and growl while walking past a playground that to his owner appears empty. This event occurs every time Jerry is taken for a walk after dark, although the behaviour is not seen during daytime walks. It is not until several days later that Jerry's owner hears laughter coming from the area Jerry has become so concerned about, and upon closer inspection he sees a group of people in the field. Jerry is able to see much more effectively in dim light than his owner and he noticed these people even when his owner couldn't. Of course his other sensory abilities such as smell and hearing also assisted him in making this observation. Jerry not only has the ability to see more effectively in dim light but also has a wider peripheral view and the ability to detect motion more effectively. This means that even if scent and sound stimuli are disrupted your dog will be able to detect aspects of his environment that you would have little hope of identifying.

This is due to a greater number of scent receptor sites in dogs' noses. Next time you feel the lead tighten, with your dog's nose seemingly stuck to the pavement investigating the ground, try to remember this. Your dog's stubborn reluctance to move past this point on the path may be heavily motivated by scent. Dogs are able to gain a huge amount of information from their olfactory system (smell) and can pick up details of their environment from a single sniff. By sniffing they are able to gain details about the environment which humans have no chance of duplicating. This has interesting implications for learning, and the dog can also learn that certain scents have positive or negative implications. For example, Chip the terrier is fearful of unfamiliar dogs. When he is out on walks he often starts to become anxious and barks and growls at certain points of his walk for no apparent reason. His owner notices that these displays occur just before a dog comes into view. Chip detects the scent of a dog before he is even able to see him, causing him to show anxious behaviour. This can be very confusing for owners but by trying to see the world through the dog's senses you can begin to understand the relevance of the dog's different sensory abilities in daily life. Problem behaviours associated with the dog's sense of smell include:

- running off after a scent and reluctance to come back;
- detecting and even stealing food;
- dog aggression (many dogs can learn to become aggressive towards other dogs and can develop a habitual fear of a specific sex, detected by smell (for example male to male);
- sniffing causing reluctance to walk fluently on the lead.

the world as search and rescue dogs and drug detectors and can even detect diseases and the onset of other health ailments such as approaching seizures, hypoglycemia and even cancer. There are, however, potential negative effects to this 'gift' in everyday life.

The dog nose is significantly more accurate than a human's at scent detection.

Most dogs find trees, lamp-posts and bushes interesting from a scent perspective.

Hearing

The dog's hearing is much more acute than that of humans (dogs hear 40-60,000HZ, humans 20–20,000HZ). Dogs also have the ability to move their ears in the direction of the sound they are trying to locate, enabling them to gain further sound information much more acutely than we can. The implications of this sensory ability for problem behaviour are vast. Problems relating to this skill include:

- noise fear and phobias (fireworks, traffic out on walks, and household appliances such as vacuums are all items that can cause your dog concern); many of these can omit higher sound frequencies which appear terrifying to the dog, although undetectable to the human ear;
- barking at passers-by or animals in the night (many of which a human could not detect).

OBSERVATIONAL LEARNING

Dogs can learn very effectively from watching their own species. Such learning can cause many behaviour concerns as dogs can easily learn both desirable and undesirable displays.

Interestingly, problems can arise not only from mimicking actions and displays (one dog barking because his friend begins) but can also be heavily influenced on an emotional level by observing problematic behaviour. For instance, if Clive the Yorkshire terrier routinely barks at strangers while out on walks, his companion dog may learn to copy and mimic this behaviour. However, depending on his temperament and other internal factors, the companion's response could be quite different: he may learn to become fearful and reluctant to go out for walks instead. Therefore it is important to remember that observational learning can influence behaviour on many levels, not simply that of mimicking. Just as Clive can teach his companion to become concerned when out on walks, a calm and confident dog could give him the self-assurance to learn a different response to the situation. Recent research has shown that dogs are also able to learn by observing the behaviour of different species, including us. This suggests that there has been social evolution among companion dogs that makes them responsive to signals you may not be aware of. This means that your dog has the ability to learn by observing your actions. It is therefore also important to consider that human actions not only have the ability to influence a dog's behaviour directly (such as pulling the neck upwards to influence a sit position) but can also have a great bearing on the dog's emotional state, with implications for calm or tense energy. For example, a person shouts angrily at their dog in a playing field several metres from where you are walking with your own dog. These shouts and tense energy have the potential to upset and stress your dog even though he isn't the focus of the angry display.

Dogs can influence each other in many ways. These two are sitting perfectly, waiting for the next command.

3 DEVELOPMENT AND PROBLEM BEHAVIOUR

Those of you currently 'battling' with your adolescent dog's behaviour can identify that as your dog goes through life you are faced with different challenges. To get through these challenges with a positive outcome you need to focus on two major aspects.

1. Preventing problems occurring by helping your dog to stay calm, confident and happy throughout their life.
2. Dealing with issues suitably and efficiently if and when they occur.

Many owners are unaware of how a dog's behaviour can change at different life stages; understanding when these changes occur, what they involve and how to manage and modify the situation is invaluable. Problem behaviour can arise at any point in a dog's life; there are, however, specific concerns which occur more frequently at certain times. In this chapter these problems will be brought to light and I will investigate which of them are most likely to occur at each stage and what to do. It's a sad fact that many owners part with their dogs as they develop from puppies to adolescents due to problems created by the change in their behaviour. This chapter shows you how to avoid this happening.

THE NEW PUPPY

Getting a puppy is an exciting time, although it is important for all owners to be aware that puppies arrive with an array of behaviours that many people may find problematic. This is not to say that living with your puppy isn't going to be an enjoyable experience, but it is crucial that you are equipped with realistic expectations and methods to cope with the challenges. This stage of development is critically important for you and your dog for two reasons.

BEFORE BIRTH

Early life experiences can shape a dog's character and behaviour. Fascinatingly, research suggests that this 'shaping' can occur even before birth. If the mother dog is subjected to stressful and negative experiences this can impact on the unborn puppies. In the foetal stage, learning does not come into play; instead, the mother's increased cortisol levels can affect her puppies' stress system, potentially predisposing them to be 'reactive' and easily stressed in the future.

1. Your dog's experience during this phase has huge implications for the 'person' he is going to be in the future.
2. You are going to have to live and deal with this dog for what will hopefully be many years; problems created now are likely to become more intense in later life.

The following list shows examples of behaviour that the puppy owner may find cute but which can become much more problematic as the dog matures. When you are encouraging your puppy to behave in a certain way, always ask yourself whether you will find these actions desirable when he is older, stronger and larger.

- Begging for or 'cadging' his owner's food
- Sitting on laps or furniture (owners of larger dog breeds must be particularly aware that they may not find a full-grown German shepherd sitting on their lap as funny as the ten-week-old version!)
- Jumping up
- Mouthing
- Biting or ragging on the lead

Helping your puppy to grow into the sort of adult that you and everyone around you will find a pleasure to live with should be a prominent incentive to get this stage right. Very few owners, however, have a completely smooth run

This puppy is ragging his owner's dressing gown. Behaviours such as these can seem funny and sweet in puppyhood but can quickly change.

with puppyhood, so dealing with issues sensitively and effectively should also be powerful motivators. Prospective owners are rarely able to have any influence over their puppy's neonatal, transitional and earliest socialization periods; it is not until the puppy reaches 'homecoming age' (approximately seven to ten weeks) that their part in the process comes into play.

LIVING WITH YOUR PUPPY: THE EARLY DAYS

The first thing to bear in mind is that your new puppy will probably have just gone through the most stressful event of his life so far, involving moving home and leaving mum. It is therefore really important to take this into consideration and make life as easy and stress-free as possible. As stated earlier, stress can be an enemy to learning, so this is the first thing to be aware of; when you come across a potential problem try to stay calm and work through it logically. The following 'Puppy plan of action' will help you to prepare and remind you of the benefits of routine and planning at every stage.

COMMON PUPPY PROBLEMS

- Inappropriate toileting
- Insecurity (reluctance to be left)
- Chewing
- Mouthing
- Fear

These are very common problems encountered by the owners of puppies and juvenile dogs, and for each one there is a suitable plan of action to help you succeed.

HOUSE-TRAINING MADE EASY

When it comes to house-training the puppy, owners are up against a few obstacles, primarily due to the infant dog's developmental stage. Young puppies (from birth to twelve weeks) are not unlike human babies: they don't have the ability to hold themselves for long periods of time when they need to go to the toilet. Hence the first part of the plan to make toilet training a success.

1. Try not to leave your puppy very long (more than half an hour to an hour) without actively taking him to the toilet area, especially after meals and whenever you see him repeatedly sniffing or circling the floor.

   Young puppies have to learn that they are supposed to toilet in a certain area (normally outside). It is true that as young canines develop they tend not to toilet in their 'den' or bed area at home, but it is important to remember that the house environment adds another layer of complication. It is probably very obvious to you and your family that your entire house is the den and not the toilet zone, but to your puppy this is a concept that even the brightest individual will often have trouble understanding without training.

2. Part two of the plan therefore involves limiting your puppy's range in the house. Avoid leaving your puppy free access to dark corners and rooms where you can't easily keep watch over him.

   Limiting access in this manner helps puppies to understand that the house is a 'clean' zone; breaking it up into smaller sections makes it easier for the puppy to learn and for you to

PREPARE

Prepare your home before your puppy arrives – ensuring all the essentials are put in place:

- Food and water bowls are ready and in place
- A comfortable bed is positioned in a quiet area of the house
- All personal items that can be easily chewed are put out of reach
- The garden is safe and secure
- Ensure you have a suitable lead and collar (with ID tag) and harness if desired; ensuring you avoid any choke chain devices!

BEGIN ROUTINE

Base your routine on your puppy's core needs and requirements such as: eating, drinking, sleeping, urinating, defecating; not forgetting exercise, play and basic training!

- Set meal times and exercise sessions
- Set time aside for play, fun and learning 'workouts' – these should be short; five minutes to begin with is quite long enough for a young puppy and ensure you don't ask too much too soon (keep it simple)
- Allow your puppy to have plenty of rest and relaxation
- Form a socialization plan; introducing your puppy to the world gradually and carefully (puppy classes are a great option to start this process in a controlled manner)

During trials of puppy ownership, try to stay calm and relaxed and deal with any issues carefully. If you or your puppy become stressed take time out to work out what is causing the problem.

- If your puppy becomes fearful of something then you will need to take a step back, reduce the intensity of what you are asking and build confidence gradually. Staying stress-aware can help you to get the best from your puppy while preventing you from missing important signals to avoid becoming frustrated and angry.

Preparing successfully for the arrival of your new puppy.

implement the plan. It is also advisable to keep your puppy in a smaller area of the house, such as the kitchen or hallway, when you are out. For a very young puppy you could even lay some puppy pads or newspaper on the floor just in case of accidents.

3. The next point of the plan involves simply and effectively training your puppy to toilet in an appropriate place. The most effective way to do this is by using positive reinforcement.

    Now that you know you must keep

A CAUTIONARY NOTE

While settling your puppy into his new home and doing the necessary training, it is vital to provide as many positive opportunities as possible for your puppy to engage with you and have fun while learning.

Limiting areas of the house should be conducted carefully; for example, Mary and Mark live in a three-bedroom house with a living room, dining room and kitchen on the ground floor. They have recently bought a puppy and a sensible way to follow part two of the plan would be to keep the dining room out of bounds and the bedroom doors shut. When Mary and Mark leave the house for a short period it would be advisable to limit the puppy's range even further, perhaps placing his bed in the kitchen or hallway. The plan does not advise you to keep your puppy isolated in a small area of your house indefinitely, or until he gets older, but aims to gradually and carefully help the puppy understand that the house area signifies 'den'. After a few days and after a walk and toilet outside there is no reason why the puppy couldn't come into the dining room to sit quietly with Mary and Mark while they are eating. The message is: pick your moments carefully!

---

actively taking your puppy to the toilet, add a command word such as 'toilet time' and ensure that you mark this behaviour with a positive reward. The reward is really up to you: vocal praise, treats and an affectionate stroke are all ways to teach your puppy that the action he has just done is correct and desirable.

4. Point four of the plan highlights the final and vitally important part of house-training, which deals with a common misconception: don't on any occasion punish your puppy if and when he goes to the toilet in the wrong place. Try to remember the reason why this occurs and bear in mind that your puppy is not being intentionally 'naughty' if he makes a house-training error – you just need to follow the basics and help him to understand what to do. If you do see your puppy showing signs that he is about to relieve himself in an inappropriate place, you can try to distract him (a high-pitched 'hey, hey' works well) and then guide him elsewhere. Just remember that punishment will not only confuse and upset him but can considerably damage your relationship.

BUILDING A SECURE ATTACHMENT AND THE CONFIDENCE TO BE ALONE

Very few owners, if any, have the luxury of being able to spend every waking moment with their dog at any stage of his life. It is very rarely a good idea to take on a dog if you work long hours and certainly not advisable to get a puppy if nobody is going to be at home for most of the day. Dogs that have learnt to be confident and secure while left alone for

Actively taking your puppy to a grassy area of your garden helps to build this association.

a few hours have an invaluable skill. This is not solely because it produces a better-behaved dog for all concerned, but because a dog that is secure and confident is generally a much happier and contented individual, free from the stress and anxiety that accompany so many less-confident dogs.

If you haven't yet fully grasped this, imagine the case of Sunny, a cocker spaniel who is very insecure. Luckily his owner is at home most of the day, which solves a large part of the problem. Living with Sunny, however, is far from easy and his lack of confidence is so great that he can't even be left behind a stair gate when his owner moves to another room only a few feet away. As soon as Sunny is unable to stay behind his owner, even for a very short time, he becomes very distressed; he barks, howls, displays extreme stress behaviour and cries incessantly. When insecurity becomes this severe it can affect every part of life with

your dog, so knowing how to help your puppy grow in confidence and security really is very important.

Your puppy's attachment to you and how it develops over time is very important in supporting confidence and security. Attachment can very simply be understood as the bond and relationship your dog has with you. Puppies in general crave, seek and give affection. They seek proximity to their owners, displaying a bond not dissimilar to the human parent–child relationship. Very interestingly, research has shown that dogs retain many of these juvenile characteristics as they develop into adults, highlighting why it is so important to help your young canine to grow in confidence and security so that he will be able to cope with periods of time without you. I have devised a 'Puppy plan to build confidence and security' to guide you through this time and help those who are struggling to get back on track.

POSITIVE REFINFORCEMENT

- Using praise and positive reinforcement methods is by far the most effective way to help your puppy develop a secure attachment with you and your family
- Avoid punishment and negative reinforcement (this can cause your puppy confusion, fear and insecurity – the opposite of what is needed)

CONSISTENCY

- All households have rules – ensure you keep yours consistent: it is futile to allow your puppy to sit on the sofa with your family and then tell him off for doing the same when visitors arrive. Inconsistency breeds confusion and causes insecurity – try to avoid this by keeping things simple and clear as change of this sort is very difficult for your puppy to understand.

TRAINING CONFIDENCE

- Start encouraging your puppy to enjoy time away from you
- Use play to facilitate this encouraging him to use toys which he can enjoy with and without you (find bally for instance)
- Begin gentle and very gradual 'confidence alone training' encouraging your puppy to stay a few paces away from you on command (older puppies twelve weeks and over are the best age to develop this further)
- Practise leaving the puppy for a few minutes behind a stair gate, then closed door, remaining in and then out of view.

Building security is very important and this diagram shows you how to do this.

DIVERTING CHEWING AND MOUTHING 'ENERGY'

Puppies commonly use their teeth for mouthing, chewing and even nipping and biting. This is predominantly because they have a great deal of tension and often even pain in their mouths when teething. Puppies also have a strong desire to explore by touch via their mouths and commonly play very roughly using their teeth. It is quite normal and natural for puppies to expend energy in this way, but things can easily get out of control. Mouthing or actually biting must be monitored, controlled and 'shaped' into other behaviours wherever possible.

There are a couple of important reasons that highlight why it is vital to conduct this shaping early on: even small teeth can really hurt and cause damage when they make contact with human skin, and this will only get worse as your puppy matures! Chewing is essential to a puppy's development and can actually be useful as a conversion tool – an important point for every owner to bear in mind. However, the important trick to being successful in this area is to ensure that your puppy chews suitable objects and not your designer shoes - no mean feat! Between four and eight months a puppy is teething – he loses his milk teeth and

the permanent teeth start to grow. Chewing also helps to align the teeth correctly along the jawbone. At this stage a dog's need to chew is so intense that he may chew any available objects, whether these are specific toys bought for the purpose, or your personal belongings. While it is annoying to find your belongings chewed or damaged, it is worth bearing in mind that these are not designed for a dog's powerful jaws, and splinters of harmful materials can easily end up in your dog's stomach, causing much distress and possibly expensive vet's bills. To avoid such disasters and achieve success in the conversion and expending of chewing energy, the following actions need to be taken.

- Keep the areas your puppy uses free of inappropriate items such as shoes, children's toys and papers. This may seem like a hard rule to follow, but it really is

This puppy is enjoying chewing on her toy.

one of the most useful and helpful to your whole family. If you don't want an item of yours to be chewed, don't leave it where your puppy has access to it.

- Provide a varied and plentiful supply of toys and chews, ensuring that these are 'puppy safe' and the correct size. Toys that are too small can be easily swallowed, which can be potentially life-threatening. If you either see or suspect that your puppy has eaten something potentially harmful, or that could cause an obstruction, it is important to seek veterinary attention. Your vet may be able to induce vomiting or retrieve the object from the stomach without surgery, but the longer the time since ingestion, the less likely this option becomes.
- Make sure that your puppy is confined to a safe area, such as a smaller area of the house (the hallway and kitchen, for example) where there is nothing he can chew when unsupervised.
- Don't forget that a suitable diet is a really important part of harnessing chewing energy. Ensure that you are feeding your puppy a high-quality feed of the correct quantity and frequency throughout the day. Adding suitable 'dog safe' vegetables such as carrots can be another really good way to contribute chewing material.

Swapping is the Key

If your puppy is chewing something inappropriate, try to get his attention without shouting at him or telling him off. A higher-pitched sound or vocal call such as 'hey, hey' can once again be useful. If the object is small and movable, such as a shoe, always swap it for something else by offering a toy or a treat instead. If you are unable to move the object your puppy is chewing, such as a table leg, use the same principle and offer an alternative object to chew on. Swapping in this manner helps to lower the value of the object your puppy is chewing, thus avoiding making him insecure or teaching your puppy that he has to guard possessions. The key is to offer the alternative object or reward but only give it to the puppy when he lets go of the original item.

HELPING THE FEARFUL PUPPY

Suitable Habituation and Desensitization

There is a great deal for your puppy to learn when you first bring him home. It is essential to expose all puppies to the 'wide world', and gradually introduce them to the many scenarios they will face. This is achieved by habituating your puppy – gradually helping him to get accustomed to key items in the environment while learning that there is no need to be afraid. The domestic dog is surrounded by potential threats to his safety, and could develop a long-lasting fear. Therefore try, for example, to prevent your puppy from becoming startled when you switch on any of your appliances, from hair dryers to washing machines.

It is also important that your puppy develops confidence and positive associations with all people, including children and visitors (so make sure you supervise introductions and any rough play!). At this point it is useful to show your puppy the car and get him accustomed to short journeys. It is critically important to carry out all habituation to new sights and sounds with care, ensuring that exposure is a gradual process. For instance, do not start introducing your puppy to traffic on a main road, because this is likely to

WHEN FEAR STRIKES

It is often very difficult for owners to completely avoid putting their puppy in a position where they become frightened. This is largely because you can't be in complete control of every experience or the actions of everybody else! Therefore if your puppy becomes very fearful towards a particular stimulus (showing extreme concern, panic and distress) it is invaluable to have a plan of action. Forcing your puppy to 'deal' with the impending fear will only cause him to develop a long- lasting apprehension to the source, creating considerable trouble for you both in the future. Many dogs that show aggression are likely to have developed this response because they were originally fearful. The following five-point plan aims to show you how to deal with fearful situations and help your puppy to overcome them.

FIVE STEPS TO HELPING THE FEARFUL PUPPY GROW IN CONFIDENCE

- If your puppy becomes fearful of something, take a step back from what you are doing and work out the source of fear. Remember that fear can strike at odd moments so watch out for any major change of behaviour.
- Try not to make a 'big deal' out of the event, and don't punish your puppy or reward him when fear strikes; simply try wherever possible to distance yourselves.
- When tackling the source of future fear, stay calm and start the reintroduction to the experience at a lower level, ensuring it is much less intensive than the one that caused the fearful reaction. For example, if the source of fear is another dog, try to find a friend or neighbour with a sociable dog and go for a walk with them, rather than head for a busy park full of dogs with unpredictable natures. The higher the level of fear, the less intensive reintroduction needs to be.
- When you come to help your puppy face the fear-provoking stimuli, break this process into smaller sections rather than tackling the issue as a whole. For example, if your puppy's fear relates to another dog, the sections could be divided into walking across a field with a dog in view, walking up to the dog, meeting the dog, walking alongside, and finally playing and interacting. During each section your aim is to help your puppy remain calm, happy and confident; if at any stage this is not the case, you should take a step back until your puppy can do it. Listen to your puppy's signals and don't move forward until you are sure that both of you are calm, confident and relaxed; this will help both of you to remain so when the intensity increases in the future.
- Don't forget to reward calm and confident behaviour when conducting any training. Use positive reinforcement throughout training (high value food treats are most beneficial). Clicker training can be another fantastic tool to positively reinforce behaviour.

'flood' his senses and potentially cause overwhelming consequences. This may lead to a fear response that can be activated when similar events occur in the future. Instead, ensure that you take your puppy to a quiet location with plenty of space to move away if he seems concerned, and acclimatize him gently. Many puppies benefit from wearing a harness when out on walks because it takes the pressure off their necks as they learn to walk on the lead.

EARLY SOCIALIZATION

It is also important that your puppy becomes 'socialized', which means learning to recognize and interact with the

The dogs in this photograph range from youngsters of five months to full-grown adults. They are involved in some rough play.

humans and other animals he is likely to meet, including his own species. Socialization is very important, because a puppy without this background knowledge and foundation training can become an adult predisposed to being fearful or defensive in such encounters. Once again the essential tool for success is to do this sensitively and gradually while listening to your puppy's signals.

Socializing with a variety of dogs is the best way for a puppy to learn how to interact with members of his own species, and also provides general games and fun. Dogs begin life with their fellow littermates and are therefore sociable from birth, but this early socialization must be maintained and developed. Even when you have successfully socialized your puppy to the humans, dogs and other animals in his life, and he is habituated to potential threats, you cannot relax your efforts, for two reasons. Firstly, research has shown that socialization and habitua-tion can wear off; and secondly, adolescence appears to affect dogs much as it does humans, and any progress made up to this point seems to get overturned! This means that you must continually reinforce socialization and habituation.

THE ADOLESCENT

Adolescence varies between breeds because smaller dogs tend to reach this developmental stage earlier than larger individuals. On average, however, this period lasts from nine to eighteen months. What happens to domestic dogs at this stage is totally confusing; just as human adolescents are heavily influenced by an influx of hormones so too are dogs of this age. The adolescent dog reaches a crossroads and many of his innate behaviours can be at odds with life at home with his human owner. Training schools and behaviourists receive many of their calls from owners of dogs of this age; so, sadly, do rescue centres, as owners struggle with the alarming perceived changes in their dog's behaviour. Their dog may ignore well-learned commands, no longer come when called, or wander away when off the lead.

It is common for owners to believe that they have been misled into buying a difficult dog, or that this behaviour is a sign that their dog is becoming defiant or establishing dominance. There is indeed a physiological change that affects cognition, but the resulting behaviour must not be ascribed to human motives. Your puppy has become an adolescent and needs a secure, controlled environment in which he can learn to be a mature adult. Adolescents require additional training and focus in their lives to give them an outlet for their developing mental and physical abilities. Fundamentally, the adolescent needs careful, kind,

Adolescent dogs can be 'scatty', selectively deaf, troublesome and challenging.

CHANGES IN BODY AND MIND

The body of the intact adolescent male dog produces testosterone at several times the rate of an adult. As a result, some male-oriented behaviour can become more extreme at this stage of life. Some dogs begin to be more defensive towards other dogs, while others become protective and territorial. The young puppy may be more inclined than the adolescent to show fear towards a threatening situation through lack of confidence and experience. The adolescent dog still experiences fear but is more likely to become defensive or even aggressive because of his psychological and physiological development. This is a natural product of these changes and has nothing to do with being 'bad' or 'naughty'; as such, it is vital to treat these dogs with understanding. The following changes accompany many adolescent dogs through their development to adulthood.

- Occasional lapses or even complete loss of attention due to raging hormones.
- As the dog matures sexually, the male begins to lift his leg to urinate. Males (and some females) begin to mark their territory with urine. This is often accompanied by an increase in sniffing behaviour, making walks on lead a challenge as every tree and lamp-post becomes a fascination.
- The female has her first season from six to twelve months, and if not pregnant may develop false pregnancies which can affect mood and behaviour.
- At around six to ten months the teeth set in the jaw and the adult teeth grow in. This means that the jaw is likely to be uncomfortable (cue chewing!).

HELPFUL STRATEGIES

Exercise such as walking on- and off-lead and mental workouts such as training and fun games will help to meet your dog's mental and physical requirements. This is very important in combating boredom and stress and helping your dog to focus when required.

It is, however, also important to be aware that some dogs can become very easily 'hyped' up and over-exuberant from bouts of off-lead running, especially if it is manic and repetitive. Be careful to keep watch for this and encourage these dogs to have regular breaks and time-out sessions to calm down. This will help to prevent them from becoming 'over the top' with other dogs or even people.

Taking your dog to training classes can be beneficial for several reasons: they give you a structure to work to, and realistic expectations; they help to socialize your dog with other dogs and people; and they provide opportunities for over-learning, which is essential for habituation and socialization. There are also many clubs and activities in which you can become involved, such as agility, heelwork to music, and many more. These can be fantastic fun for owner and dog alike; such activities are also great opportunities to exercise your dog both mentally and physically, and to help meet his requirements.

Play between adolescent dogs can get a little 'over the top' and excessive, as these two friends are displaying.

considered and sympathetic handling. They do absolutely require structure and control but this does not need to be carried out by force in order for you to be successful.

COPING WITH THE ADOLESCENT

Regard this life stage as a period of 'over-learning', so that for every command that your dog appears to have forgotten, you return to the way you first taught it.

Four Simple Rules

- Make sure your dog gets something out of each training session – praise, a reward, or fun. You can use your dog's toys as rewards and doing this will encourage your adolescent to play both with and without you. Don't be afraid to ask him to go and find his favourite ball and play with it.
- Present training as fun and keep it lively and upbeat. If things begin to get out of control or a little over the top, keep calm and slow the pace of training. Even encouraging your dog to pause for a few seconds can help.
- Be patient: getting annoyed won't help either of you and if you find yourself getting aggravated, take a break. Training can be exasperating at times, so try not to be too hard on yourself or your dog and be realistic in your expectations.
- Keep your training sessions short – fifteen minutes maximum – and set small and simple goals to ensure that progression is easily achieved.

ADOLESCENT PROBLEM BEHAVIOURS

Some of the most prominent problems that owners have with their adolescent dog's behaviour are ragging activity, boisterousness, and an inability or reluctance to concentrate and 'do as they're told'! As we have seen, the motivation for this

---

CASE STUDY

Max is a year-old German shepherd who has become increasingly 'mouthy' towards his owners as he has grown from a puppy. This behaviour was encouraged when he was a youngster but is now routinely and severely punished. This has made the concern a great deal worse and Max has even begun snarling and growling when his owner begins to use force. Max is highly stressed through the routine use of punishment, which is making him increasingly tense and 'mouthy' through the release of this energy. Additionally, when Max is handled he regularly holds and mouths his owner's hands in expectation of further rough handling, thus encouraging them to let go of him. This is a cycle that needed to change as somebody was going to get hurt and relationships are very fragile.

The key to changing Max's behaviour was firstly to stop the use of violence, which was not only making Max acutely stressed but was adding to the mouthing problem. The next step was to convert this energy into something else and ensure that Max had a plentiful supply of toys that he likes to play with. At any stage of mouthing, Max's owners needed to convert this energy into something else, even asking him to do behaviours such as a simple sit and give paw for a reward. The resulting modification was almost instant and Max continued to develop into a much better-behaved dog.

behaviour is largely down to hormonal influence, and it is really important to remember this. Adolescent dogs are challenging and can really try their owner's patience. It is very easy to lose your temper and become angry, which commonly results in worsening or more extreme behaviour because the dog is not capable of understanding the emotional implications of its actions. To get through this stage successfully, therefore, you must try to remain calm and confident and use 'brains over brawn' rather than starting battles that nobody can win.

PROBLEMS: COPING, MANAGEMENT AND MODIFICATION

When dealing with a boisterous adolescent don't be afraid to allow him a 'crazy five minutes' to run around and release some energy – but probably open the door to the garden and encourage him to do this outside! Punishing this behaviour is going to make your dog increasingly wound up, and the key to helping him through it is to get him to calm down and relax in order to use his brain effectively. Asking him to go through a repertoire of simple commands such as sit, down and give paw can be an excellent way of calming the brain. You can develop this further and practise target work and mat training (*see* Chapter 5). The same applies to the mouthing or nipping adolescent, and if the swapping or diverting energy rules are not working, the next step is to stop what you're doing and get your dog used to offering a different behaviour by making him think and putting him to work. An excellent way to deal with the dog that is reluctant to do as he is told relies on two things: timing and finding an easy alternative behaviour. Remember, rather than simply telling your dog what not to do, tell and encourage him in what he should be doing! The case study of Max shows how to do this.

4 ENVIRONMENTAL CAUSES OF PROBLEM BEHAVIOUR

The first three chapters showed how health, learning, development and life stage influence the occurrence of problem behaviour. At this point it is vital to investigate the critical part that exterior influences have to play. External influences cover your dog's environment, lifestyle and the treatment he receives. If any one of these three components is at odds with what your dog needs, then it is very likely that this will contribute to undesirable displays. If you can become aware of these fundamental causes and have the knowledge to modify them, you can successfully shape problem behaviour and prevent things from going wrong in the future, while stopping the same mistakes from being repeated.

YOUR DOG'S NEEDS

As we have seen, every living being has a set of core needs that must be catered for in order to survive. These core needs or maintenance behaviours cover eating, drinking, sleeping, defecating and urinating. Additionally there are needs that are specific to a species and also to the individuals within it. All dogs as a species require food, water and sleep, but individual requirements for different dogs can vary greatly. This is where dog breed or 'type' characteristics are important to consider; for example, the average border collie requires a high level of exercise, whereas the pug may need much less demanding exercise. In order to meet your dog's needs at all levels, it can be really useful to look at them separately to see what can happen when individual requirements are jeopardized. Try to visualize the problems you are having as you review the following 'needs' table to see if any of the behaviours shown familiar.

This dog h
restrainin
out.

NEEDS (CORE AND SPECIES/ INDIVIDUAL)	HOW THESE CAN BECOME COMPROMISED	CONSEQUENCES
DRINKING	• Water deprivation	• Severe implications for internal state and survival will be under threat within days
EATING	• Food deprivation/ not fed enough • Unsuitable diet for the individual (not considering age/ development or physical expenditure)	• Severe implications for internal state and survival will be under threat within days • Lethargy • Irritability through low blood sugar • Protective/aggressive behaviour displayed around food items (resource guarding) • Steals food • Low body weight and disruption of development/ creating physical and psychological future concerns • Hyperactivity or lethargy depending on weight stage • High body mass • Irritability • Inability to exercise effectively thus compromising another need (particularly overweight dogs) • Severe implications for medical health (for example: diabetes, joint problems) • Mood swings
	Sleep deprivation auses: stress, environment ange or pain	• Acute and chronic stress On edge/frantic/manic displays of behaviour or lethargy/ depression • Aggression/irritability Internal state compromised as the body and mind are unable to repair or process information effectively • Stereotypical behaviour Severe implications for survival and behaviour and welfare if prolonged sleep deprivation continues
	cerns can prevent or cation in this area	• Pain • Irritability and mood swings • Aggresssion • Survival compromised

EXERCISE (PHYSICAL AND MENTAL STIMULATION)	• Lack of exercise	• Overactive behaviour • Excess energy • Problem behaviours such as: boisterous, manic, mouthy, destructive, excessive attention seeking, OTT displays • Boredom • Overweight body condition
	• Too much or unsuitable exercise	• Physical exhaustion • Pain, injury, weight loss/low body weight • Lack of energy • Lethargy • Reluctance to go out • Irritability and potential aggression through stress and threat or further pain or fear of event • Mental exhaustion • Excessive and repetitive running/frantic exercise can cause stress – over active and manic displays (mental exercise is needed as well!)
ATTENTION	• Lack of attention – left alone for long periods in isolation	• Insecurity • Anxiety when left alone • Attention seeking
SOCIALIZATION	• Lack of socialization with people and other dogs can lead to concerning behaviour	• Frustration • Inappropriate greeting behaviour • Problem behaviours: fear/aggression through lack of social skills/interaction

The importance of catering for your dog's needs and the consequences if any of these are compromised.

COMMON PROBLEMS WHEN NEEDS ARE COMPROMISED

When any one of the dog's maintenance behaviours (survival needs) is compromised, this can very quickly cause considerable concern. This is fundamentally because it makes the dog acutely stressed through his inability to cope with what is happening, often because survival could be under threat. This is caused and created by an internal imbalance within the dog, who must act in order to survive. Interestingly, owners are often faced with the 'side effects' of this occurrence, which tend to show up as problematic displays and undesirable behaviour. When the dog's general needs and individual requirements are jeopardized, a very similar pattern appears – it may just take a little longer. Problems that manifest include:

- Fear
- Stress
- Aggression
- Depression
- Hyperactivity and under-activity.

This list covers a very wide variety of problem behaviours that precisely match the most common issues that face owners. From this you can understand not only the importance of this aspect of environmental influence, but also why a suitable lifestyle is so vitally important for your dog.

CASE STUDY: HENRY

Henry the retriever has always been afraid of loud noise. He lives with his family in a city suburb and was becoming increasingly stressed with the approach to Bonfire Night. As the first bangs began, Henry started to become extremely anxious and upset – so much so that he was unable to sleep for four days. On the fourth day his gentleman owner walked past him and accidentally stepped on his paw. Henry yelped and snapped at the passing leg. This was the first time he had ever displayed any aggressive behaviour, but he was tired, on edge and acutely stressed. His reaction was a likely by-product of the emotional upheaval he is experiencing.

The principal point behind this case study is to remember to give your dog extra space and consideration when he is stressed or tired; consider that his behaviour may become out of character if his internal levels are unstable. This brings me to another point: when stress strikes it is even more important to provide a safe place for your dog to hide away. A covered crate, left open, or even a thick blanket for him to snuggle under can be very useful.

CASE STUDY: PEPPER

Pepper was an eleven-month-old neutered male beagle. He was purchased from a breeder as a ten-week-old puppy and as he approached adolescence his family had considerable problems with his boisterous and extremely active behaviour. Pepper spent the greater part of his day confined in the hallway of his home and was separated from the family regularly even when they were present. This was largely due to his active displays, jumping up, and mouthing behaviour. Pepper didn't have a regular exercise regime and didn't have access to a garden, and this, together with his routine confinement in a small area of the house, inadvertently contributed to his activity levels because there were no physical and psychological outlets available. Therefore when Pepper was released from the constraints of the hallway he displayed increasingly active, frustrated and manic behaviour, which progressively intensified. Punishing treatment added to the manic nature of his actions and he started to become defensive and aggressive.

The key to unravelling this situation involved starting a new, modified exercise routine and training in the house to stop the cycle of undesirable behaviour. Pepper needed rules to follow so that he could understand what he was supposed to be doing, but he also needed to have his individual requirements met. Tackling the concern at both ends resulted in a transformed dog in a very short space of time, and highlights how important it is to ensure that your dog's needs are being met when addressing any problem behaviour. In this way the key to changing things may be much easier than you think!

Similarly, many problem behaviours can be misunderstood as naughty, dominant or challenging actions; often (understandably) this results in the owner using punishing and sometimes severe treatment to try to solve the problem. It can be really beneficial to see how these misunderstandings translate into real life. The following case studies will show you how easily such events can occur, and reveal that in spite of the owner's first conclusions, a dog's appearances and expressions of behaviour often originate from a very different cause.

Even though there is a huge amount of variation between dogs all over the world, as an owner you can cater for their core requirements by remembering the points addressed so far. This doesn't have to be complicated; the table [below] highlights how to cater for these needs, and offers tips on what to do when things go wrong.

It is important to remember that often the happiest and best-behaved dogs are those whose environment caters for their basic needs and personal requirements. Interestingly, these range from the fundamental survival necessities right through to exercise, socialization, attention and instruction.

DIFFERENT BREEDS, DIFFERENT DOGS, DIFFERENT NEEDS

Exercise

Dogs need mental and physical exercise and are likely to suffer physically, mentally and behaviourally if they are not given enough. Inactive dogs can become overweight, which can cause stress to joints, ligaments and tendons. For the large majority of dogs, letting them out in the garden is no substitute for a walk.

Not being walked can affect dogs in several ways.

Firstly, they aren't able to go anywhere new and this can lead to boredom and frustration. Remember that even routine walks are different each time for dogs, because the sights and smells of whoever has passed by change. Taking your dog to a new area adds to this diversity even more. This variety and interest can't be replicated in the garden alone.

Secondly, dogs who don't go out for walks cannot practise and learn how to behave outside the home environment. Even adult dogs must continually learn that outsiders of all species are no reason to be concerned. Being deprived of the outside world can result in problematic displays: social skills can become 'rusty'; frustration and pent-up energy can produce over-the-top and rough displays; and as a result, owners and other walkers and dogs can become defensive towards your now troublesome canine. This often results in a downward spiral of behaviour as your dog spends less time off-lead, outside and exercising, which in turn often makes the whole problem much worse. The key is 'keeping it up'! Remember that re-socializing an aggressive dog needs special care; we shall look at this in more detail in Chapter 9.

Thirdly, dogs naturally follow others, canine and human alike, as part of their genetic disposition. Dogs restricted to garden-only exercise don't have the opportunity to use this trait to its full potential. Following you round the house and garden is very different from following you climbing stiles or walking through the woods. Outside walking, in particular off-lead running, allows you to take turns on who is leading the way, turning onto paths and retracing steps as you choose. It's one of the best ways to

DAILY NEEDS			FACILITATING NEEDS	WHAT TO DO WHEN PROBLEMS HAVE ARISEN?
Maintenance	Feeding		• Ensure your dog is fed a high quality feed which is suitable for their age, sexual status, exercise level and behaviour. • Be aware that some dog foods can cause certain individuals to become prone to 'overactive' and manic displays through the additives they use. This is not dissimilar to the effect sugary products and additives can have on children. Therefore look for a high-quality feed that is ideally free from unnecessary additives and preservatives. There are some fantastic hypoallergenic feeds on the market that can really help to avoid contributing to underlying problems.	Food guarding is a principal problem associated with feeding and can be very serious (will be discussed in more detail in Chapter 9). These tips aim to practically help alleviate the problem by shaping the feeding routine: • Give multiple feeds: feeding twice and even three times a day (same quantity only split) can help to make your dog feel fuller for longer. This can help to lower the value of food while you begin changing the relationship your dog has developed. • Try to give the 'resource-guarding dog' chews and treats that he can eat in one sitting rather than guard. Smaller treats and chews are a good alternative over large bones which can raise guarding potential.
	Drinking		• Always provide dogs with water.	• I have seen dogs develop very odd behaviours associated with drinking; some that involve patterns of avoidance/showing a reluctance to drink. Add new water stations as well as the principal water area to give the dog plenty of opportunity to drink.
	Sleeping		• Ensure the dog has a safe, quiet place where they can rest without disturbance day and night. A crate left OPEN at all times with a towel covering it can make a fantastic den for dogs to retreat to.	• Disrupted sleep patterns can play havoc with dog and owner alike. Alleviate concerns by setting modified routines to cater for the individual. • Ensure the dog is not too 'het up' before bedtime

		• Ensure all members of the household (especially children) allow the dog time to rest whenever it needs to do so.	by active fast walks if prone to excitability. Calm training, relaxation and mat work can be useful in helping your dog to reach further stages of relaxation any time of the day (for more see Chapter 5).
	Urinating & Defecating	• Don't just wait for your dog to ask to be taken to the toilet. Allow him access to this area frequently throughout the day, actively taking him at points as well. Ensure that he is taken as late as possible before being confined and as soon as you return/get up in the morning; remembering that dogs don't have the luxury of freely being able to go to the toilet inside whereas you do!	Any sign of concern – inability to go to the toilet or excessive toileting behaviour (urination or defecation) the vet must be consulted straight away. Once medical causes are eliminated: • Go back to basics and start retraining toilet association ensuring you consider any recent stress/change that has occurred recently and may need modifying. • Avoid punishment as this will only make matters worse and is not an effective way of tackling toileting concerns.

How to cater for your dog's needs, and what to do to regain control and harmony.

develop bonds and learn about each other, especially about ways of communication. Remember that dogs have evolved as our companions in many ways, but much of this partnership has become ingrained through outside living, hunting and socializing. If you can tap into the natural disposition and drive that is specific to your dog, it can be a very effective way to combat many causes of problem behaviour.

Walks in the outside environment are mentally and physically stimulating; especially off-lead play and socialization with other dogs. Exercising helps the dog to use his legs and muscles, which can be a fantastic way to relieve stress energy. Taking your dog to new places with different environments and varying sights, smells and textures, such as woodland, fields, streams and beaches can be a great way to engage their investigative abilities. Stressed and fearful dogs often stop investigating because of the tension they are feeling. Taking dogs to areas rich with places to explore is a wonderful way to use this natural behaviour. However, this advice comes with a cautionary note for owners of fearful and under-socialized dogs: build the intensity of outings

This dog is exploring a river flowing through woodland; her alert ears and head posture display this perfectly.

and introductions carefully and gradually. It's important to seek out quieter areas to build confidence before moving on to more intensive, busier areas. Trips to a quiet lake and woodland are likely to be more beneficial than a stroll along a busy nature trail.

Your dog's individual exercise requirements will vary depending on many factors such as age, breed type, physical disposition, health and personality. Requirements are also likely to vary as your dog matures. There are some dogs who are happy and content with two twenty-minute walks a day, whereas others quite simply seem to be impossible to tire and would be happy out in the fields all day.

In each of the Kennel Club's seven breed groups there are dogs needing high levels of mental and physical exercise. In fact, there are relatively few breeds that require low levels, and the majority of these fall into the toy breeds category, including dogs such as the chihuahua, Chinese crested, papillon and

Dog breeds traditionally used and selected for working purposes, such as springer spaniels (pictured), are generally very active.

Socialization offers opportunities for dogs to exercise (often very actively), release stress and learn from each other.

pug. Miniature dachshunds are also examples of dogs that require lower levels of physical exercise because of their petite stature and physiology. Breeds that have been used for working purposes over the years are prime examples of dogs needing higher quantities of exercise. The most active dogs include working breeds such as collies, shepherds, terriers, rottweilers, boxers, malamutes and huskies, utility breeds such as dalmatians and akitas, and the large majority of the hound breeds. These dogs need an active life, with an abundance of exercise opportunities and variety to keep them happy and content.

As a general rule a quick ten-minute lead walk once a day is not going to be adequate because these dogs have been specifically bred and selected over generations to have an active mental and physical make-up. Breaking walks into two or three sessions a day can be beneficial from both a physical and a psychological perspective, and I have found this a very useful tip for the large majority of owners struggling with high-energy dogs. Off-lead exercise and play sessions with other dogs are another way to cater for their needs. If your dog is a singleton, finding a regular play friend or walk mate to go out with can be very useful.

Additional lead walks to the shops for family shopping trips are another way to keep your dog consistently using his brain and body. Training sessions are another good way to top up exercise, with short (ten to fifteen minute) workouts teaching new behaviours and going through the ones he knows. Play is another valuable tool for all dog owners and offering plenty of opportunities to play with toys is definitely advisable. Encouraging your dog to play alone as well as joining in fun games together is also a good way to build security. Tugging is instinctive for dogs, as it is a co-operative act in group feeding. It also engages the mouth and front legs, which is why dogs enjoy playing 'tug of war'. I would, however, avoid playing this game with resource guarders and dogs that are

Providing your dog with a variety of toys gives him additional opportunities to investigate, play and exercise.

prone to 'ragging' the lead. Swapping items and games of fetch make good alternatives and are much more suitable. Young children should never play this tugging game as it is all too easy for the dog inadvertently to catch a finger in his enthusiasm.

TRAINING, TREATMENT, AND YOUR BEHAVIOUR

Owners whose inappropriate training leaves dogs fearful and confused or mentally and physically frustrated can cause great disruption. It is therefore vital to investigate the next important aspect of the environment which affects your dog on a daily basis: the treatment he receives. There is no denying that problem behaviour can be exasperating

for owners. There are many trials, tribulations, threats and pressures for the owners of 'problem dogs', and a vast array of emotional consequences. However, of all the components of your dog's environment, the one over which you can have the greatest impact and control is your own behaviour. I cannot emphasize this enough: the relationship you have with your dog is vitally important and influential for his actions. The concept of attachment status will help your understanding.

Attachment Status

Attachment can be simply understood as the bond and relationship that you have with your dog. Although attachment was first used to explain the bond of affection that develops between a human infant and its caregiver, it has since been recognized as applicable to many social species, including dogs. Laboratory tests have found that the dog's relationship to humans appears similar to a child–parent relationship. This is because the behaviours demonstrated in the test situations could be categorized along the secure–insecure attached dimensions, as in human mother–infant interactions. A secure attachment is essential for a baby to develop into a psychologically healthy adult, and there are also important implications for dogs. The level of attachment your dog has with you and other members of your family can be directly influenced by what he has experienced in the past, and what he will experience in the future.

There are four categories of attachment: secure attachment, and three forms of insecure attachment (avoidant, ambivalent and disorganized). A dog with a secure attachment status is happy to have close contact with people, even

The attachment you have with your dog has great bearing on your overall relationship.

those he does not know very well. A dog with an avoidant attachment may be reluctant to approach people, let alone be handled. The attachment you have with your dog is a very important aspect of understanding why he behaves in a particular way.

Dogs that have a secure attachment status are likely to express mostly favourable behaviour, with consistently friendly greetings, yet show the independence to be secure playing on their own. Dogs that have an insecure attachment vary in the three ways listed above, but generally do not like being left alone, are 'clingy' and 'needy', and may show other concerning behaviour. Thus an insecure avoidant dog may choose to avoid human contact altogether and may be very reluctant to approach you; an insecure ambivalent dog will show varying degrees of greeting behaviour, at times friendly and affectionate, but also showing defensive behaviours alongside

PROBLEM BEHAVIOUR: A THREAT TO HUMAN CONTROL?

Problem behaviour consists of actions that are undesirable for a wide and varied number of reasons. However, there is one component that governs all issues. Problem behaviour disrupts and threatens human control. As a species humans in general like to be in control and when this is in jeopardy it can cause a huge amount of stress, not only because loss of control can lead to potential danger but also because it can threaten perceived authority. This is why the identical problem behaviour in two different dogs with different owners may cause amusement in one home and anger in the other. You will find a deeper insight into the implications of dominance hierarchies in Chapter 7. For now I want to highlight the importance of keeping calm and managing behaviour problems in a relaxed, intelligent manner in order to unravel the real reason for them.

these greetings. An insecure disorganized dog shows random and extreme greeting behaviour and can be of real concern. The implication of this information is quite simple: don't underestimate the importance your behaviour and actions can have on your dog and the relationship between you.

Negative Reinforcement and Punishment v. Positive Reinforcement

Chapter 2 discussed positive reinforce-

This dog is motivated to jump up on the table by the possibility of a tasty morsel. This is a natural behaviour that is undesirable, but dogs are not capable of understanding why this behaviour is wrong.

ment as a means of increasing the frequency of a behaviour by rewarding it. Giving something good or pleasurable to the dog when he acts in a particular way helps him to learn very effectively, supports behaviour that you find desirable, and makes it more likely that your dog will offer these actions in the future. I hope that having reviewed the importance of attachment status and how insecurity can cause many problem behaviours, you have now begun to query the true effectiveness of using non-positive reinforcement methods of training. The big question, however, remains: what should you do when your dog behaves in an undesirable way, displaying behaviour that you perceive as bad and problematic? It may seem logical that if it's important to reward desirable or good behaviour, then you should punish undesirable or 'bad' behaviour. Unfortunately, and fortunately for the dogs whose owners understand this, it is just not that simple, because of (a) a dog's cognitive ability and (b) the way dogs learn.

The dog's cognitive (psychological) capabilities of understanding are not the same as those of humans. Dogs are not capable of understanding why certain behaviours are wrong. A dog can learn to associate certain actions with negative consequences (which explains why some cower before their approaching owner after they have carried out an action that has previously been punished), but this still doesn't mean they understand it. Critically therefore, dogs lack the ability to learn effectively from punishment and certainly tend not to offer any new or positive behaviours from its extreme or constant use. This explains why so many dogs that are punished for a specific behaviour carry on repeating it, leaving their owners totally bewildered as to why they 'haven't learnt'! If behaviour is motivated by internal and external components such as the way the dog is feeling and the environment he is in, then the type of behaviour expressed is highly dependent on these 'causes'. When this expression results in undesirable actions and punishment is inflicted, the behaviour may be reduced or even extinguished at that moment in time, but it does little to deal with the root of the problem. In fact, when a behaviour is suppressed it often has no place to go, and may be released and expressed in other (often undesirable) behaviours or create internal problems. In severe cases individuals in this situation may appear defeated, shut down and depressed, and can often become the most difficult and worrying to cope with. At this point outbursts of extreme behaviour are possible through the eventual release of the pent-up energy and distress. Displacement behaviours and stereotypical actions can also occur as by-products of suppression and punishment and the stress that governs them.

This should help you not only to understand your dog's problem behaviour and actions more clearly but also to deal with them correctly. It is very difficult to extinguish all use of negative reinforcement; however, if you only take one thing from this discussion, I hope you will remember that your dog simply can't understand punishment in the way that humans can. Using positive reinforcement, however mild, is greatly beneficial to everyone and produces much truer and continuous development than does momentary and fleeting suppression. If your dog is doing something undesirable, using distraction as a tool and quickly rewarding the good action can work much more effectively

---

THE VALUE OF VARIETY

You should randomize positive reinforcement training so that your dog receives different levels of reward and doesn't expect and need the highest value each time in order to perform the command. It can be useful to save higher-value treats and food for the actions that are hardest to train, and even randomize these and lower their values over time. Voice, affection, stroking and contact, and clicker/treat reinforcement can be used and varied at different times. Avoid using clicker training at times of complete relaxation as it may over-stimulate the dog's brain. It can, however, help to shape your dog's behaviour up to that point, and then a change of tone can support the next desirable action, which in the case of relaxation training will be sleep. A quiet 'good boy' or 'good girl' will be more suitable at this stage. The goal is to be able to ask for a behaviour and receive it the first time it's requested. This may take time to perfect, but the key to doing it is continued and correct practice and reinforcement (see 'super-training' in Chapter 12).

---

than losing the trust in the relationship through harsh and continued punishment.

Clicker Training: A 'Magic' Tool

Clicker training uses the principles of classical and operant conditioning and positive reinforcement, providing a truly powerful trio of training tricks! The clicker (a small box that makes a clicking noise when pushed) is superior in its effectiveness in marking desirable behaviour because the quick, sharp noise is easily recognized by the dog, and when paired with a treat becomes exceptionally powerful. The treat you use is entirely up to you; however, I recommend using very small amounts of food for each treat and randomizing their appeal. Voices can get lost in a dog's mind, because they hear huge variations of talking throughout the day. When the clicker is introduced as positive reinforcement, it signifies unmistakably to your dog that he has done something desirable. When a food reward is paired with the click sound, the dog experiences additional positive reinforcement as his brain releases a chemical reward, dopamine, in anticipation of a treat. When the dog actually eats the treat this acts as another positive reinforcement, explaining why clicker training can be such a useful tool.

HOW THE CLICKER WORKS

I find clicker training an invaluable method of positive reinforcement because when used correctly (in conjunction with a reward) it not only helps the dog understand what constitutes 'good behaviour' but also helps to support positive emotions. It can be a key to unlocking many of the behaviours you thought were untrainable and is particularly useful for owners of 'problem dogs', and for counter-conditioning when you want your dog to learn alternative behaviour. The crisp and clear 'click' sound is used to mark good behaviour and supported by a food treat as double reinforcement. When the dog hears the click (after previous pairing) he understands that this action is favourable, anticipates a food reward and then receives it. Timing is important and for the most effective use, ensure you 'click' on the good behaviour.

Before you begin clicker training, you must ensure that your dog is not afraid of the sound. If he is, then you may be doing more harm than good if you use it straightaway, as it will become a punishment rather than a reward. If your dog is concerned, it will take time to remove his fear and it is important to remember that some dogs, such as those phobic to certain sounds, may not be suitable for this training. To begin clicker training, gradually build association starting with a very quiet clicker or dulling the sound in a jumper or coat. If your dog is not afraid of the noise you can begin 'clicking and treating': throw a treat on the floor and as the dog gets close to the food, 'click' and he will then eat the treat. Repeat this until your dog connects the click sound with food.

The next phase involves giving your dog simple commands, preferably ones he already knows, and each time he follows the command correctly, click and treat. If you repeat these commands a couple of times, you are not only reinforcing these behaviours, you are also teaching the dog that the sound of the clicker means he has got it right. Keep these sessions brief (ten to fifteen minutes) with regular breaks because your dog needs to experience consistent success.

This dog is responding well to the clicker reinforcement and is waiting for the next command.

5 STRESSED OWNER, STRESSED DOG

Very few people, if any, will have gone through life without experiencing the effects of stress and the significant impact it has over feelings and behaviour. Similarly, stress can have huge implications for your dog and is the cause and result of many behavioural problems. Unfortunately, stress is contagious, and owners in daily interaction with stressed and problematic dogs can very easily reach a similar state. This chapter takes a practical look at how to identify, manage and modify stress, while examining its relationship to day-to-day behaviour. Problem behaviour can cause a cycle of stress generation, which becomes difficult to break; my aim is to show you how to change this.

WHAT IS STRESS?

There is in fact good stress (eustress) as well as bad stress (distress) and it's important to remember that sometimes even so-called positive events can cause a stress response. In this chapter I am particularly focusing on the 'bad' variety. This is much more likely to occur when a dog goes into the instant alarm state; the body can only sustain this position for a limited period before something is likely to occur that causes concern. Stress is a mental and physical reaction to danger, real or otherwise, short or long term. The brain and body switch into action to deal with the situation, activated by psycho-logical stressors such as fear and anxiety and physical stressors such as pain and extremes of temperature. Once an alarm state is processed, the 'flight or fight' mechanism is activated. This is useful in the short term for direct threats, when the individual can act upon its influence; but badly adapted to long-term scenarios or when action is not possible. For example, if your computer crashes an hour before an important deadline and you are unable to fix the problem, it is likely to cause you stress. A lead restraining a dog under attack from another can produce a very similar physiological reaction. Stress is increased in both examples by the organism's inability to take any action to deal with the situation.

Whatever the cause, the stress response is an innate ability that helps the body to take appropriate action to maintain homeostasis (keeping temperature, blood pressure and so on at a constant level, regulated by the hypothalamic-pituitary-adrenal axis) and thus survival. Although a dog's physiological response to stress is comparable to that of humans, there are clearly differences in the perception of 'stressors' and capacity to cope with them. Another point worth remembering is that some dogs, just like certain people, are more effective at coping with stress than others; this is an important consideration when approaching any behavioural problem and how to tackle it. The next important step in helping you understand this process is to take a look at what causes stress behaviours, both short and long term; what do they look like when they occur? You can't tackle stress if you don't know what it looks like; many of the signs can be easy to miss, so it is vital to begin here.

ACUTE STRESS (THE SHORT-TERM MECHANISM)

Put simply, all mammals have two main types of nervous system: one for regulating the body at rest, aiding digestion and relaxation (parasympathetic); and one for regulating the body when in action (sympathetic).

When your dog experiences acute stress his body reacts with a short-term mechanism to deal with the situation and potential danger. This is controlled by the autonomic nervous system. Examples of acute stressors that you may have come across include:

Threatening events such as this rather aggressive display by the collie on the left can cause stress.

- Noise (door slamming, fireworks)
- Confinement (being kennelled)
- Travelling
- Attack or threat of attack (dog or human instigator)
- Restraint
- Handling (particularly if the dog has contact concerns)
- Extremes of temperature (being left in a hot car)
- Separation
- Frightening objects, people or animals approaching
- Harsh training methods using pain and punishment.

Acute stressors jump-start the stress reaction, which is why dogs react so quickly to a threatening situation. Additionally, as discussed in Chapter 2, the dog's differing sensory abilities enable him to notice and process details much more acutely than humans can, often leaving owners puzzled as to the problem. For example, the dog's highly developed and acute olfactory system (scent) and acute hearing mean that they can detect other dogs or people approaching often before they can see them. Such situations can totally bemuse owners, as their dog's behaviour comes out of the blue and they have no notion what triggered it. This is why gaining an insight into what stress signs look like in the dog can be so useful, together with practical knowledge of what to do when you see them.

Acute Stress Signs and Behaviours

Acutely stressed dogs reveal their state of mind and body by various signals. These can help you to know when your dog is becoming concerned about a situation, which is invaluable when working out what to do next. Imagine Jed, a collie who has just been bitten by another dog and

ACUTE STRESS 'FLIGHT or FIGHT' (The short term stress mechanism)

INTERNAL EFFECTS

- Hormones released to sustain the body for action. Primary stress hormones are cortisol and adrenaline released by adrenal glands affecting and regulating:
- Metabolism (energy production)
- Blood pressure/body temperature increases
- Blood directed away from digestive system to feed the muscles
- Insulin released to balance blood/sugar levels
- Immune/inflammatory response increases

BEHAVIOURS POSITIVE/NEGATIVE (eustress+/distress–)

The longer acute stress continues the higher the chance distress will occur. The body can't sustain acute stress for long without negative implications.

- Alertness/enhanced cognitive function (memory)+
- Quick supply of energy to enhance performance/run faster or fight harder/helps sustain ability+
- Reduced sense to pain+
- Feel hot/agitated/off peak performance–
- Inability to concentrate/distracted–
- Shaking/trembling–

(REMEMBER BOTH POSITIVE AND NEGATIVE EFFECTS OF STRESS FOR THE DOG INTERNALLY CAN HAVE NEGATIVE EFFECTS FOR BOTH OWNER AND DOG IN THE MODERN WORLD)

Acute stress influences dogs internally and externally.

whose body is internally preparing him to react in the most effective way. He displayed several stress signs when the dog bit him and became acutely stressed by this event. Moreover, due to the learning process, he is very likely to show similar stress behaviours on the sight of this dog in the future. If you can correctly read and understand his signals you can help to diffuse the pending tension in your dog.

THE FLOW OF STRESS ENERGY

When examining stress and the effects it has on you and your dog, it can be really useful to visualize it as an energy flow. Try to imagine a dog in a relaxed state calmly lying down for a stroke by his owner. Picture his flow of stress energy, how low and steady it is, without spikes and increases. This dog is currently regulated by the rest and relaxation pathway and all is calm. His body is relaxed, face soft and round, and he is cool, with no sign of rapid panting or frantic movement. Now imagine a car backfiring outside, which alarms both owner and dog and makes them jump into action. Imagine the stress energy within the dog not only increasing but flowing rapidly throughout his body, quite literally influencing his every breath. Now his body is tense, face furrowed and eyes wide; because of the increase in temperature and blood pressure he is panting rapidly as more energy is produced to help in this potentially dangerous situation.

The stress energy that flows through the body must go somewhere and it is filtered into behaviour as the dog consciously and subconsciously sees fit. If this dog's options are limited, either by restraint, boundaries or immobility, imagine the disruption this is likely to cause his natural response. Without an outlet, this pent-up stress energy can result in conflict such as displacement actions, which are normal behaviours occurring out of context at an abnormal time. Additionally, redirection behaviours are likely to be presented such as snapping, biting or lunging towards the cause of restraint. Try to imagine this energy escaping through these actions as the disrupted flow builds and boils over into many undesirable displays. Stress is energy and it can be very useful to remember this whenever you come face to face with its influence.

The five dogs in this photograph are meeting for the first time. Each dog is under lead control, which can contribute to the stress reaction through the restraint it causes.

STRESS SIGNS (acute and chronic)	WHY IT OCCURS
Heavy panting (not necessarily after exercise)	Increase of blood pressure and body temperature causes increased panting to cool down through stress hormone production
Tongue ridged and tense and often held low out of the mouth	Part of the panting process to lose heat but with added tension through tightening of muscles. This is different from the dog panting purely because he has been exercising as in these cases the tongue is often 'floppy', hanging loosely out of the mouth
Facial ridges	Tightening of the muscles causes facial ridges to appear
Wide eyes	Eyes and pupil dilate to gain as much information about the situation as possible
Tight lips ('sucking a lemon' expression)	The tension in the muscles adds to this expression
Shaking/trembling	Adrenaline causes the muscles to contract
Whining	Communication
Stereotypical behaviours (repetitive actions with no obvious function such as spinning)	Coping mechanism potentially started as displacement behaviours to release stress energy (caused by acute stress rise but often presented when chronic stress is present)
Barking	Communication vocal (stress release)
Increased urination/defecation	Hormonal influence on digestive system
Sweaty pads	Increase in temperature

The presenting signs dogs show when stress strikes, and why they occur.

CAN OR CAN'T COPE?

Coping Mechanisms: Calming Signals and Displacement Behaviours

Dogs have several techniques for combating, communicating and releasing stress energy that often include calming signals and displacement behaviours. There is a certain amount of overlap between these two 'types' of behaviour although, as a general rule, calming signals are directed towards outsiders such as the owner or another dog, and displacement actions, such as sniffing their own genitals and drinking or gulping water, are directed inwards. For example, when Sally the

The collie in the forefront of this photograph is acutely stressed. His eyes are wide, pupils dilated, face furrowed, tongue ridged and wide at the base, and body tense. He is also showing a paw lift (or calming signal to diffuse tension).

labrador is at the vets for a check-up, she lifts a paw and starts lip-licking with her eyes focused on the vet as he bends down to examine her (calming signals); Terry

The terrier on the ground is displaying a protruding tongue directed towards the dog on his right. His feelings of concern are likely to be a reaction to the black dog standing over him.

the dalmatian repeatedly goes back and forth for a few laps at water from his bowl during the arrival of visitors in his home (a displacement sign). Calming signals include:

- Yawning
- Paw lift
- Slow movement and freezing
- Tongue flicks and lip-licking
- Sniffing the ground
- Avoiding eye contact, sitting or lying down (stomach on the floor)
- Turning away and turning back
- Urinating.

Calming signals are the dog's universal language for defusing conflict. These signals may help to reduce the dog's tension physiologically but they are also signals that communicate their state to other dogs, animals and people.

Displacement behaviours include:

- Drinking, lapping and gulping water (out of context)

- Sniffing
- Scratching
- Yawning
- Urinating
- Stretching.

Many displacement behaviours occur as an outlet for stress energy to 'fill the gap' that is produced when the dog's natural or desired actions are not available to them. For example, Chippy the Jack Russell is fearful of unfamiliar men. While out on a walk with his owner, a male stranger approaches wanting to give him a stroke. Chippy is on the lead and although he is fearful his owner insists that he remains still to be handled. Chippy communicates several calming signals towards the man and tries to move away, but as he is unable to do this he begins to repeatedly sniff his genitals.

Remember, dogs may show a combination of intentional and unintentional signs that reveal how they are feeling. Try to make the effective observation of these subtle signs second nature. You will be amazed at how much you learn from your observations and find that you can have a much greater impact on how your dog feels, and consequently on how he behaves.

CHRONIC STRESS

Chronic stress is stress that occurs frequently and potently over time. When a dog becomes chronically stressed he may not get the chance to reach a balanced internal state because he is seldom regulated by the parasympathetic nervous system (compromising true rest and relaxation).

This trio are displaying several displacement behaviours and calming signals: scratching, looking away, and tongue protrusion.

Jess, an active and sensitive German shepherd, has been placed in a particularly noisy kennel environment for several months. She is likely to become acutely stressed initially, but regular and continuous bouts of short-term stress can add up over time, eventually producing a chronically stressed individual. This type of stress can have a severely negative impact on behaviour and welfare. Chronically stressed dogs, like human beings, can become extremely depressed and troubled; when the body is subjected to stress in this way it can cause many health concerns. Therefore, the chronically stressed dog is very likely to have behaviour problems and is in real need of help. Additionally, a chronically stressed dog is much more likely to react to stressors of any kind because the internal imbalance prevents their brains from processing or coping with what is occurring. This is why such dogs continue to display an abundance of acute stress signs when they have reached this high level. Remember also that even dogs in a seemingly normal environment can become chronically stressed. Changes that are beyond a

Change of environment can cause dogs acute and chronic stress, particularly if the new surroundings are at odds with their needs.

dog's control, such as the arrival of a new baby or a new house guest, can create stress.

Examples of chronic stressors are:

- prolonged threat to any of the dog's maintenance behaviours
- change in environment (such as being placed in kennels or the introduction of a new dog in the home)
- punishment and pain (such as harsh training methods used frequently over time)
- separation
- noise
- inability to move.

Many acute stressors occurring frequently and potently over time can result in a chronically stressed dog.

Signs of Chronic Stress

- Fat accumulating around the abdomen; an abundance of the stress hormone cortisol causes belly fat to build up and fat cells to get larger.
- Disruption in sleep patterns (absence of effective rest and time to process information or repair the body).
- Reluctance to eat or over-eating, caused by frequent disruption to the digestive system by all the hormones in the body.
- Reduced immunity that predisposes the dog to frequent bouts of illness.
- Dry, scaly and itchy skin through immunity disruption.
- Grey hair growth or loss of hair.
- Stereotypical behaviours (actions which are repetitive with no obvious function).
- Inability to concentrate and learn new behaviours.
- Frantic behaviour.

For chronically stressed dogs, stress behaviours are often presented throughout much of their everyday waking life. Such individuals present habitual stress signs and are often over-active and manic, and regularly appear unable to cope. Some may have shut down altogether and

---

A DAY IN THE LIFE OF A STRESSED DOG

Jonas is a six-year-old male labrador that has been in and out of the rescue environment for two years. When Jonas is calm and relaxed he is extremely friendly with dogs and other people both in and outside the home. Jonas becomes acutely stressed when he sees male strangers approaching; this causes whining, barking, lunging and displays of aggressive behaviour. When he is approached by a man while on a walk, his stress levels increase considerably and for the rest of the walk he is highly reactive to anybody passing by. However, if Jonas is not directly approached, he can pass people without concern. The important message behind this example is that stress can dictate the way your dog behaves from one day to the next, depending on the events that occur.

If your dog becomes stressed, he is much more likely to react to another mild stressor even if this appears to you to be of no real concern. This is the nature of the stress process in dogs and explains why even the simplest of days can be a minefield for the stressed dog, and you can be caught out by a behaviour display for which you were totally unprepared. The important message to remember is that when stress strikes, ensure that you are extra aware of your surroundings and begin to gain your dog's focus in order to control, calm and maintain balanced levels.

PROBLEM BEHAVIOUR RESULTING FROM STRESS	WHEN THESE PROBLEMS COMMONLY OCCUR	HOW TO START TACKLING THE CONCERN
Inappropriate toileting	• 'Scary' events/people or dogs can cause urination (sometimes even defecation) through fear/stress of danger	• Note what causes this reaction • Be very careful to prevent the dog in this position from practising the behaviour wherever possible • Lower the intensity of the interactions and desensitize at HIS level, gradually building confidence and exposing to the stimulus at the level he can cope with (*see* Chapter 8)
Mouthing	• During 'episodes' of high stress the energy is often released through the mouth (visitors arriving) • Can also occur when handled especially if the dog has concerns (stress caused) with contact	• Keep calm and direct the mouthing energy to something else – ask the dog to do something • Replace shouting 'no' with a command such as sit and then reward. Use toys to deflect chewing and mouthing energy also (*see* Chapter 10)
Inability to listen/focus and learn; often over-active and fanatic behaviour is seen	• This is a by product of the stress response and is likely to occur whenever stress strikes	• Work through relaxation and calm training • Mental training sessions can be useful in helping the mind to focus
Re-direction (snapping, biting, lunging towards lead/other dog or restrainers, such as owner's hands or legs)	• Often occurs when a restraint is in place, such as owner holds dog (the lead is also a common restraint to cause redirection)	• Don't restrain dog with hands/feet; especially avoiding bending down and putting yourself between your dog and the point of concern • Circle away/use toys/other items and even treats to regain focus and reward calm behaviour when it is achieved

Inappropriate vocal displays such as barking, high-pitched whines and cries	• Commonly occurs on sight of a 'threat'/through anxiety	• Try to remain calm/circle away and regain focus • Work on gradual desensitization/counter-conditioning (train a different response to the stimuli) (*see* Chapter 11)
Inability to be left alone/undesirable displays presented such as: howling, barking, destruction of household items, toileting	• Commonly occurs when left alone/left in a different room	• Work on building attachment status (bond and relationship the dog has with you); independence and confidence • Start plan of action for separation-related problem behaviour (*see* Chapter 10)
Stereotypical behaviour	• Through spike of acute stress in a chronically stressed dog when the dog can't cope	• this is a severe stress concern that needs careful assessment. Important a vet is consulted first and then supervised training can begin to reduce stress wherever possible and and retrain the response (*see* Chapter 10)

There are various common behaviour problems that relate to stress. This table reviews these issues.

seem to be in an almost 'zombie' state. Such dogs can become welfare cases and veterinary attention is certainly needed as soon as possible.

UNDESIRABLE BEHAVIOUR AND PROBLEMS ASSOCIATED WITH STRESS

Stressed dogs can become extremely difficult to live with. Some dogs will become increasingly active, while others can become depressed, listless and unsociable. Now that we have examined the appearance of stress, including what to look for, it is vital to see how it influences some common problem behaviours in dogs. The next section shows you how to help your dog to combat stress in everyday life.

STEREOTYPICAL BEHAVIOUR

Spinning, wall-licking, tail-chasing, self-grooming, shadow-chasing, fly-catching, water-staring, digging, wall-jumping and chronic pacing are all examples of behaviours that can become stereotypical. Stereotypical behaviours are repetitive and often compulsive actions displayed with no obvious function. They can be stimulated by the dog's natural disposition and often mimic different parts of the dog's predatory sequence such as eye, stalk, chase and bite, and so on. I have seen dogs from a wide variety of situations display such behaviour, from pedigree German shepherds bought as puppies to rescue dogs in and out of the kennel environment. When stereotypical behaviour occurs in the home it can be particularly worrying. The key to helping dogs overcome these issues lies initially in understanding why they as individuals are acting in this way.

Why?

Stereotypical behaviour can be the product of boredom and frustration and is most commonly linked to stress from this and other causes. Displacement behaviours are often produced when the dog experiences emotional conflict, but when this intensifies he can begin to show repetitive behaviours to defuse the tension he is feeling. The trouble is that these actions then become self-rewarding and teach the dog to behave in this way both in times of stress and (in severe cases) even in normal everyday situations. Stereotypical behaviour can be related to seizures and epilepsy but can also be completely behavioural in its cause. Nevertheless, it is a worrying and potentially hazardous concern and owners can even be bitten if they to try to handle the dog and interrupt the behaviour. Some dogs have been injured by these repetitive actions; others have even emptied their entire water bowl and needed their owners to refill their bowls repeatedly throughout the day.

What to do: An Action Plan

Firstly, a visit to the vet is essential, followed by a consultation with a behaviourist to ensure the best course of action for each specific case. The following action plan aims to help you manage and support you dog.

- Don't punish the stereotypical actions. This will lead to further stress and intensify the dog's need to act in this way. If this behaviour could also be a product of attention seeking, try not to give it; diverting this energy before you think the behaviour is likely to occur can calm emotions.
- Reduce stress wherever possible. Identify the times the actions are displayed and ensure that you take extra care to keep your actions and dog's environment calm and relaxed. Introduce new calm areas; an open crate, an extra bed and even an old towel can be useful target zones.
- Introduce clicker training. Relaxation work such as mat training and the calm command (explained later in this chapter) will help to tackle the underlying stress. Remember that clicker training increases the production of dopamine, the feel-good chemical that can be extremely useful in combating stress. Additionally rewarding the dog in this manner can provide him with valuable positive emotions and encourage him to display alternative actions. Over time this makes a reduction of the stereotypical actions much more likely.

- Reward the dog for calm relaxed behaviour (especially when it's shown at times when the stereotypical actions often occur).
- Find an outlet for your dog's energy and give him simple tasks to do that will curb the behaviour and direct it into desirable actions. Target work (going to a mat) for a reward and simple tricks can be a great way to start this; but remember that calm is the word!

THE STRESSED OWNER

A DAY IN THE LIFE OF A STRESSED OWNER

Mark and Sally own Betty, a young female springer spaniel, and have recently had a baby. They are overjoyed by their new arrival although, like any new parents, they have many sleepless nights ahead of them. Betty has always been a fantastic dog, but like many of her age and breed she is very energetic. She has always been inclined to jump up for attention; at first this was merely annoying for her owners, but when the baby arrived home the jumping up continued and this time was met with much sterner actions. Betty's owners started to become increasingly stressed by her behaviour and this created a cycle of insecurity.

The stress began to grow and was passed on from owner to dog and back again as the behaviour displays got worse. The more Betty was pushed away, the more insecure she became and the more demanding her behaviour and the frequency of her jumping. Betty and her owners were locked into a cycle of stress. Stress grows and is transferable between humans and their dogs – a fact that is really useful to remember.

Stressed Owner, Stressed Dog?

A direct relationship exists between the reactions of owners and their dogs; stress can affect this balance significantly. Owners can unwittingly make the situation worse by engaging in a whole battery of automatic responses. When your dog becomes stressed you are likely to tighten your hold on the lead and generally become tense. You may even start to vocalize instructions with increasing volume as you feel you are losing control. This often confirms your dog's belief that his concern is justified. He may even feel he has to defend you!

This highlights why it is important to be aware of your own behaviours and try to stay as relaxed and calm as possible. The absence of human stress will certainly reduce the intensity of a stressful interaction and will help you to remain focused rather than emotional. Dealing with a stressed dog can, at times, be really difficult, so ensure that you take regular breaks yourself and if you are going round in circles or becoming angry, try to take a few minutes for 'time out'. Focus your thoughts and picture what you want to achieve while bearing in mind the nature of the stress process. You can achieve success but it is vital to remain calm wherever possible.

HELPING THE STRESSED DOG

The first stage of helping a dog suffering with stress is to work out precisely what is causing this reaction. To begin this process I have designed a questionnaire to help you identify what is going wrong and when. It is also very important to remember that breaking the cycle of stress generation may require a 'spring clean' of stressors, especially in relation to your dog's core needs and mainte-

What behaviours can you see? (List the stress behaviours)	When do they occur? (List exactly when you see them)	How often do they occur? (Does the behaviour occur every time?)
Example 1: • Heavy panting Wide eyes/pupils Barking	**Example 1:** • When male strangers approach	**Example 1:** • Only occur when male strangers with hats on approach
Example 2: • Shaking • Heavy panting • Whining • Reluctance to eat • Frantic activity	**Example 2:** • When left alone in a room with the door closed • When in a crate with the door closed • When we leave the house	**Example 2:** • Every time
Example 3: • Drooling • Trembling • Urinating • Spinning • Wall-jumping • Will not accept treats • Barking	**Example 3:** • When kennelled for holidays after a week	**Example 3:** • Every time

This table can be adapted to your own situation to throw light on what your dog's 'stressors' are.

nance behaviours. The disruption of any one of these may be the principal cause of the stress that faces you. Before completing this questionnaire make certain that you have taken care of your dog's drinking, eating, sleeping, urination and defecation needs.

As mentioned in Chapter 1, it's also absolutely vital to ensure your dog receives a full check from your vet to exclude any medical reasons behind the problem behaviour. Once this is complete, the second phase comes into play. This is where you must try to break the stress cycle by preventing your dog, wherever possible, from practising this reaction. Remember, it is always very important to consider the thresholds of stress; the more stressed your dog becomes, the easier it will be for him to become stressed. Therefore once you have discovered what the stressors are, you can begin to work out how to reduce the incidents.

Calming the Mind and the Body

Helping your dog to feel calm and relaxed is something that can't be valued enough, and we shall be looking at helpful techniques in the next section. In so many behavioural problems, helping the dog to remain relaxed and diffusing his stress can have a huge effect. The stress reaction begins when stressors are processed by the dog; the most effective way of combating this is to help your dog to remain as relaxed as possible throughout the day and ensure he has regular periods for rest and recuperation. Helping your dog to recover more effectively each time from 'bouts' of stress energy is also an extremely useful method of beginning to shape his new way of living.

STRESS MODIFYING TECHNIQUES

The calm programme

The principle behind the calm programme is helping your dog to regain calm and relaxed emotions when at home. The programme works by training the dog to adopt a position that automatically engages the parasympathetic nervous system, and consequently helps him to feel calm and relaxed. Never force the dog into this position, as this would have the opposite effect and cause his muscles to tense, which could be potentially hazardous. It is a training system to encourage the dog to relax and take all-important 'time out' and can be really useful for those dogs who habitually engage in stress behaviours.

How to Train the Calm Command

- The starting point is 'sit'. Ask your dog to sit in a quiet area of the house where he can relax (in front of the sofa is a really good place for this as you can remain sitting beside him). A mat, dog bed or even a towel can be beneficial as a target area for him to sit on, so make it as comfortable as possible.
- The next step is to use a treat (if needed) to guide the dog from sitting to lying. If your dog knows how to lie down on command this will be useful, but don't worry if he doesn't as this

Once your dog is calm and confident in a sitting position, guide the head lower to the floor, encouraging a down position.

could be the perfect time to teach him. Try not to manoeuvre him into position with your hands as this is very invasive and not conducive to relaxation. Always guide rather than force as this is less stressful for everyone concerned.

- When your dog is lying down, use the 'calm' command and repeat it while offering a treat to guide his head lower; encourage him to lie down and roll onto his side. The aim is to have the dog as low and relaxed as possible – his legs can be stretched out and he can be lying flat out on his side. There are many variations depending on the individual: some dogs will not like to

When your dog really starts to relax, encourage him to move over to his side and fall deeper into a relaxing position.

lie flat out, so use your judgement to determine your dog's calm position.

- Feed treats as low as possible, below the level of the heart, to help to relax the body and therefore the mind. Reward him with soft vocals and gentle stroking; this positively reinforces him for shaping his behaviour to this command, and he is also learning that being with you is a pleasurable experience.
- If you feel resistance to the command, don't worry. Take a step back and try again later. Just standing in one place and focusing on you for thirty seconds can be beneficial for dogs that find being still difficult.
- Don't use clicker reinforcement when the dog is really beginning to relax as it can have the opposite effect and heighten his arousal levels. When the eyes become soft and begin to close, stop and replace clicker with gentle stroking and calm, soft vocals as stated before.

Mat Training

Mat training is an additional method for building relaxation and concentration. You can train your dog to associate the mat with safety, a place where he can feel at ease. This means that you have a useful tool for calming your dog when visiting friends, or when you have to take him with you on more serious occasions. The mat itself should be made of a warm material that is both comfortable and comforting for the dog. Fleecy materials are good, and a thermo backing is ideal so that the cold of the floor cannot strike through. You can also move a mat around to various locations when you are trying to build stationary training.

Once again it is important not to manoeuvre your dog with your hands, but shape his behaviour so that he understands what is required. Shaping has the added advantage of being an effective mental exercise for your dog. But remember, little and often; take a break after five to ten minutes, or if your dog is starting to lose concentration.

- The aim is to teach your dog to have a positive association between the mat and safety.
- The mat should be large enough for your dog to lie on it without spilling over the edges.
- First reward him for being near the mat, or for touching it with his nose or feet. Achieve this by guiding him to the mat, giving the command 'mat' and rewarding him when he puts a paw in the right location.
- Repeat this exercise until he has effectively understood the principle – that is, when he goes to the mat area on command. Once this has been established, ask your dog to sit and even, when he is totally happy in this area, lie down.
- To begin with, make it easy for your dog to learn this command by standing in front of the mat. Use the word 'mat' while standing further away, and reward him for going to this area.
- Then begin to increase the distance you are standing from the mat when you give the command. Looking or pointing at the mat will help to communicate what you want your dog to do.
- The next stage is to see if your dog can learn to reach the mat and then lie down for the one command 'mat'. Although many dogs can pick this up quickly, there are those who do not, so take it slowly, with frequent breaks. Don't be afraid to allow your dog to

offer the desired behaviour now and again without being given any cues or commands. This may take several tries but really helps the dog to use his brain as he works out what he needs to do to gain a reward.

- Never punish your dog if he doesn't do as he is asked: this would defeat the purpose of the exercise, which is to teach him how to relax. This can only be achieved by using positive reinforcement along the way.
- The next stage is training your dog to stay on the mat area. This begins by asking your dog to 'stay', and then pausing for a couple of seconds, and if he has remained still, rewarding him. If he jumps up or moves instead, ask him

Mat training requires practice and the dog in the photograph is practising a perfect sit, targeting the mat.

In this photograph the dog is staying on the mat at a distance from his handler.

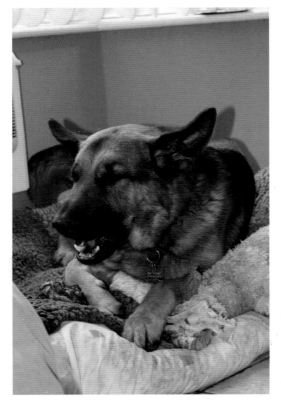

Chewing is important for dogs and can help them feel calm and relaxed by expelling energy and producing feel-good chemicals in the brain.

to do something simpler. This will also help to develop the command you are trying to teach.

- Once again, don't worry if he doesn't get it first time. The training is supposed to be fun and enjoyable for both of you.

Once you can get him to 'stay' for a couple of seconds, begin increasing the time, from three seconds to four to five, and so on. At this point stay in the same place and do not move away from him. When he can stay on the mat for thirty seconds, you can begin increasing the distance you are from him. This is harder, as your dog may really want to be with you, so move away only one step at a time. Reward every time he does what you are asking. Once again, if he doesn't do what you ask, go back to a step he can do, and reward him when he achieves success.

CONVERTING STRESS ENERGY

Mouth Work

Many stressed dogs release this energy from their mouths and can develop a habit of holding, grabbing and biting their owners. This mainly focuses at hands, arms, legs and clothes, as well as household items such as carpets and furnishings. Although boredom can also be a cause of such problems, the mouthing is often accompanied by other stress signals. Below are some suggestions for conversion items and methods to help with this problem.

- Chews: for the dog, chewing has several very positive effects. It activates feel-good chemicals in the brain that aid relaxation (remember the parasympathetic nervous system), and also enables the dog to lose tension energy through the mouth.

- Toys: mouthing, holding, pushing and playing with toys can dramatically help in reducing stress and tension in dogs. Offering the dog a toy instead of an arm can also help to avoid confrontation and prevent additional stress from developing.
- Suitable diet: ensure that your dog has the right quantity and quality of food for its size, breed and age.

EXERCISE FOR THE STRESSED DOG

It's absolutely vital that all dogs have an adequate exercise routine suitable for their age, breed, status and health. It is often impossible to tire a stressed dog and owners find that the more exercise he has the more hyperactive the dog seems to be. The reason for this lies in the dog's psychological state; these dogs simply can't switch off their brains, due to the active consequences produced by the stress pathway. If you have ever had difficulty getting to sleep because you just can't 'switch off', you will appreciate how the dog feels. The solution is to ensure that you not only give him exercise for his physical needs but also exercise his mind: for example, going through simple and basic commands one after the other can help the dog to focus rather than run around chaotically. Offer regular bouts of mental training such as toy games to add variety and interest within exercise sessions. Activities that focus the dog's brain rather than allowing it to run manically can really help stressed dogs to remain cool and collected instead of spiralling out of control. Don't be afraid of trying out calmer and more focused games as well as more active ones.

Encouraging your dog to take breaks when playing can be useful to stop manic and hyperactive play getting excessive.

6 SECOND-HAND DOG, FIRST-HAND PROBLEMS

Providing a loving home for a rescue dog can be a rewarding experience, because you can watch the transformation in a dog that might not have had a chance without you. There is such a diversity of dogs in rescue organizations all over the world that prospective owners should be able to find a dog specifically suited to their lifestyle, which is not always the case when buying a puppy. Forget the common misapprehension that rescue dogs are the second class citizens of the dog world; they can and do make fantastic companions. It is, however, important to enter the adoption process with your eyes wide open, because the rescue dog can pose specific challenges.

Rescue dogs come in all shapes and sizes with varying temperaments and characteristics.

It is important to be realistic: some dogs are in need of new homes because they have become unsuitable for their current owners and may even have 'baggage' in the form of behavioural concerns. The good news is that one family's nightmare dog is another person's ideal friend, although many rescue dogs undoubtedly need some extra help settling in, and some behaviours are universally problematic. This chapter aims both to prepare future owners of rescue dogs and to show dog owners how to identify, manage and modify problem behaviour resulting from change and upheaval in a dog's life.

RESCUE DOG BEHAVIOUR

Are Rescue Dogs Different?
How your dog behaves and, indeed, misbehaves is the result of a complex set of processes which can be broken down and simply understood. Your dog's emotions, reactions and choices are influenced by internal factors such as his genes, health and hormones, and external factors such as his environment and experiences. If we consider these factors and apply them directly to the rescue dog, we can gain some insight into the problem.

Firstly, these internal and external factors are not permanent, and specific changes in both categories are brought about by the rescue process itself. A prime

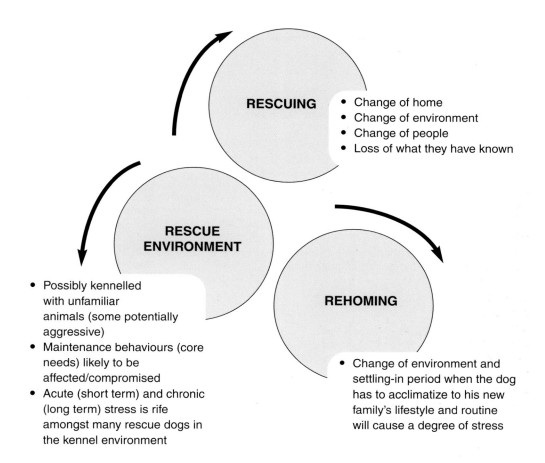

RESCUING
- Change of home
- Change of environment
- Change of people
- Loss of what they have known

RESCUE ENVIRONMENT
- Possibly kennelled with unfamiliar animals (some potentially aggressive)
- Maintenance behaviours (core needs) likely to be affected/compromised
- Acute (short term) and chronic (long term) stress is rife amongst many rescue dogs in the kennel environment

REHOMING
- Change of environment and settling-in period when the dog has to acclimatize to his new family's lifestyle and routine will cause a degree of stress

However a dog comes to be a rescue dog, entering this process and environment can have implications for behaviour.

example is that many dogs are spayed and neutered in rehoming centres, which changes their hormone production and the behaviours that depend on it. Additionally, as anyone who has visited a rehoming centre will testify, this environment can be a far cry from a home. The kennel situation can give rise to a well-researched condition known as 'kennel stress', and while this need not be long lasting, it makes it difficult to know the true nature of a dog suffering from it.

However, it is always important to remember that every dog is different; some dogs are able to cope more effectively with change and the stress it brings than others. Fundamentally, though, it's the changes fashioned by the rescue process that lie behind many behavioural concerns.

IMPORTANT QUESTIONS TO ASK ABOUT A PROSPECTIVE DOG	IF THE ANSWER IS NO	IF THE ANSWER IS YES
WAS HE A STRAY?	Try to gain as much information as you can about his history such as: • Who made up his last family? • How many homes has he had? • Why was he handed in?	The results of a behaviour assessment and the carers' findings will be able to help you gain extra information.
DOES HE HAVE ANY BEHAVIOURAL CONCERNS?	This is a good start but remember: it is important to be realistic – most dogs will require some further training to help them acclimatize to your lifestyle and particular requirements.	Don't panic but ensure you find out details about the concern. It is important to discuss the implications of this behaviour and stay realistic. Ensure that you consider how this behaviour will affect you and if this is going to be a problem.
IS HE SOCIABLE WITH ALL PEOPLE, CHILDREN AND ANIMALS?	Find out who he is specifically unsociable with. The relevance of this will depend upon your family situation, where you live and who comes to visit and how often.	You are likely to have found a very special dog although it is important to remember that you must continue this socialization; ensure he continues to build positive experiences with people and animals alike (this is especially important for puppies and younger dogs that are still developing, and remember even a well-socialized dog can change if it experiences a fearful or traumatic event so care must be taken).
IS HE HOUSE-TRAINED AND HAS HE REMAINED SO IN THE KENNEL ENVIRONMENT?	Find out if he has ever been trained. If the dog have never lived in a home so will need to be house trained and it may take a little longer to complete.	This is encouraging but ensure you begin a house-training routine nevertheless; establish appropriate toileting behaviour as soon as he arrives home.
HAS HE BEEN RETURNED?	This may mean that you are going to be the first home he has had since being in the kennel environment.	Try to find out why he was returned. Remember it may have not been his fault but if the return was the result of a behaviour problem it is very important to know so you can be prepared.

These important questions can help you to be prepared for what you can expect when you take your dog home.

RESCUE AND REHOMING

The rescue, housing and rehoming process affects every dog passing through the system. Additionally, it's often very difficult to know how the dog will behave in everyday life. This means that many owners may not be aware of any potential behavioural problems until their dog arrives home. This being the case, it's important to try to gain as much information about the dog you are intending to rehome before signing on the dotted line. This should enable you to accurately judge and interpret the behaviours your new dog presents; and, as discussed earlier, this is very important when deciding how to tackle everyday problems successfully.

Homecoming and Settling In

For many rescue dog owners the settling-in period can be a breeze, leaving these lucky families feeling confident, content and set for the future. For others this period can be fraught with stress and anxiety; some owners even contemplate returning the dog. It can take several weeks, months and sometimes longer for rescue dogs to settle into their new homes, and some behavioural problems can arise during this time.

A sudden change of environment can be a source of stress and uncertainty in a sensitive dog. It is also unlikely that your dog has developed the trust and confidence in you that would help him through this change. This can lead to the dog suppressing his normal behaviour and exhibiting one of two contradictory outcomes.

1. He becomes quiet, potentially fearful and cautious.
2. He becomes overactive, with manic displays. Overactive, somewhat juvenile displays of behaviour can also occur when the dog begins to settle in and grow in confidence.

Once again your dog's nature will dictate his coping capacity and the behaviour he displays will differ accordingly.

Problems with settling can also revolve around the dog becoming accustomed to the 'house rules'. This can be a cause of friction between many owners and their dogs, so my plan for this crucial stage includes tips to make the settling-in process as smooth and successful as possible by avoiding, managing and modifying potential problems.

COMMON RESCUE DOG CONCERNS

Breaking the Rules

Some owners love to have their dog sitting on the sofa beside them, while others wouldn't ever consider such a thing. It is not difficult to imagine the confusion and distress experienced by a poor rescue dog who had previously been encouraged to sit on the sofa, but is now told off for doing exactly that.

This is just one example of how a dog can easily and unknowingly break the house rules during the settling-in period. It is imperative to remember that your dog may actually be completely unaware of your rules rather than deliberately challenging and naughty. What is more, the way you handle these situations has dramatic implications for future behaviour and can be the source of many additional problems. This highlights the importance of knowing how to cope with the problems facing you, especially in the first stage of settling in, when early impressions and experiences

BROKEN HOUSE RULES	REASONS	SOLUTIONS
Sitting on the sofa	• Because it is the most comfortable place to sit! • Accustomed to this behaviour in a previous home/been encouraged or even trained • Eager to get as close to owner as possible/desires to give and receive affection • Potential insecurity • Desires to sit as high as possible potentially to keep guard and watch surroundings (out of window) or to feel more confident due to fearful/nervous disposition	• Avoid physically manoeuvring him – especially if you don't know each other very well or if he is fearful or nervous • Instead encourage him to come 'off' the sofa for a reward such as a toy or even treat (when he does just this and not before!) • Try not to push him away if he jumps on your lap as this can contribute to insecurity • Instead work on teaching 'targeting' other areas/ alternative seats close by on the floor. An old towel, blanket or dog bed can work well for this purpose
Jumping up on work tops	• To investigate • To keep look out • To find food • Anxiety (particularly if left alone)	• Ensure surfaces are kept clear and keep room out of bounds if possible when you are not there to supervise • Ensure food is NEVER left on the work top otherwise you are positively reinforcing the problem behaviour every time the dog receives some food for doing just this. This 'trade off' is extremely high for some dogs and can fuel a much stronger desire than punishment. Some dogs will over ride punishment to get to the food • If the problem relates to anxiety further training will be necessary
Not allowed to go upstairs/certain areas	• Is not aware that this behaviour is not allowed • Used to free access in a previous home • Desires to be with owner at all times	• Swap confrontation for management and if you do not want your dog to have access to a certain area ensure he can't access it to begin with (i.e. with stair gate)

	• Desires to keep watch on higher level	• Develop stay and wait training and teach your dog to stay in a certain area or not to go any further into another
Barking when the door bell rings/ knocks	• He may have been trained to do this in the past by a previous owner • Insecurity • Nervousness • Habitual 'territorial display'	• This can be a difficult behaviour to modify if he has been practising it for some time so remain realistic, it may take training to modify • Begin 'door-bell training' to shape his reaction • Many dogs that display this behaviour are reflecting a 'protective drive' therefore may be a little insecure of people invading their home. Punishment will not help tackle the cause so avoid shouting or punishing the dog for being noisy as it will make him worse!
Begging for food	• Hunger • Used to obtaining food from past owners this way	• Never feed him from the dinner plate! • Ensure he can't steal the food from you

Some rescue dogs have been encouraged to exhibit behaviours that are totally undesirable to their new owners. The table shows this.

are very important for everyone concerned.

House-training

Inappropriate toileting is a frequent behaviour among rescued dogs, particularly during the settling-in period. Stress can cause dogs to become anxious and confused and if your new dog does not understand where he is supposed to go to the toilet, accidents will very easily happen. Consequently it is really important to start the house-training routine as soon as your dog arrives home. Bear in mind that he will not be familiar with his surroundings, so actually take him into the garden on the lead and allow him to have a walk and sniff round. Hopefully he will go to the toilet and when he does, ensure that you praise him and let him know that this is good behaviour. Repeat this action every one to two hours to begin with, especially after meals and before bedtime or periods when he will be left alone. The golden rule is not to punish your dog if he goes to the toilet in the wrong place. This will not help the situation and can make matters much

TEDDY BREAKS THE RULES

Teddy is a two-year-old terrier cross who was rehomed from a rescue organization after a short time in kennels. When Teddy arrived in his new home, he spent a good deal of time investigating his surroundings and getting to know his new house. His new owners were pleased to see he was confident wandering around the house and sat down on the sofa for a tea break. Seeing this, Teddy rapidly moved to where they were sitting and jumped up on their laps, not knowing that this was against the rules in this house. He was, therefore, picked up and put on the floor straight away. Five attempts later his owners were still following the same cycle: Teddy jumped on the sofa and was picked up and put on the floor. Several attempts later, tempers naturally became frayed, voices were raised and two sets of hands grabbed Teddy and attempted to push him down. He reacted to this with a very aggressive display, growling, lunging and snapping at the hands holding him. The combination of raised voices, anger and two sets of human hands grabbing him became too much and produced a defensive display of aggression. His owners were obviously very shocked and upset at this reaction, particularly as they had only just brought him home.

We had no knowledge of Teddy's previous home and the past experiences which may have shaped this response, but it was fairly clear that Teddy had been accustomed not only to sitting on the sofa but also directly on people's laps. Furthermore, during the first few days he displayed insecure behaviour, frequently seeking contact and affection. Interestingly, although he craved such affection, he also showed concern when handled in certain areas, specifically his rear end. Teddy and his owners had not yet built enough trust and confidence in each other for such direct handling, and many dogs would feel threatened with contact of this sort. Once his owners became aware of his problem behaviour they took time to find an alternative method of 'sofa training' that did not involve manoeuvring him physically. They also concentrated on developing mutual trust between them. The most interesting aspect of this case study is that there was more than one cause of the problem behaviour and one problem led instantaneously to another.

This dog has taken to sitting happily on the sofa; some rescue dogs may have been used to doing this in a previous home.

KENNEL DOG OR HOUSE DOG: BREAKING THE DIVIDE

Some rescue dogs have never lived in a home, while others, such as ex-racing greyhounds and some working dogs, have spent their entire lives in a kennel environment. There are also neglected dogs who have been so confined that they had no choice but to go to the toilet in the same area, even if this meant on their bed! While it is not surprising that this can occur as a result of neglect, this is often the situation in so-called 'puppy farms'. For dogs such as these, house-training can be even more difficult to pick up, mainly because they have no understanding or experience of going to the toilet in a different area from the one they identify with their 'bed'. Training and modification of inappropriate toileting for these dogs follows the same principle as before but may have to be carried out a little more rigidly.

ACTION PLAN

- Keep calm but start a fixed house-training routine from the second the dog comes home – don't wait for things to go wrong.
- Always use the same lead for taking him to the toilet so that he comes to associate it with the action.
- Ensure that this lead is as long as possible (flexi leads work well for this) as this will encourage him to circle and sniff.
- While in the garden, take him to shrub and tree areas and walk him amongst the undergrowth.
- When out on walks take him to areas used frequently by other dogs.
- Give him time to sniff around (and don't forget your bags for picking up afterwards!).
- Go back to the same area each time you want him to go to the toilet.
- Separate the house into sections when he is left alone and don't let him have free run of the house until house-training has been established (he may still think one room is his bed area and the next room is the toilet zone, especially if he has never experienced a garden).
- Praise, and then praise some more, when he goes to the toilet in the correct place (and use plenty of tasty treats).

Stair gates are a great way of dividing areas of your house and avoiding having to confine your dog to a very small space (crate), which can cause concern.

89

worse. If you do catch him sniffing an area repeatedly and circling it with head low and intense concentration, quickly make a distracting noise and recall him in a bright and friendly tone so that he will come to you and you can take him out. If you shout at him or worse, he will not want to come to you and may even avoid you altogether. Furthermore, you will have taught him that sniffing and circling will lead to punishment, so you are unlikely to see him doing it again. Undoubtedly, this will make the problem increasingly severe.

Another related problem can occur with a male dog who will probably try to mark this new area with a lift of a leg! This does not mean that you will need to follow him everywhere, suspiciously jumping into action at his every movement, but it is advisable to prevent him from going unattended into areas where valuable furnishings are located.

NERVOUSNESS

You can tackle nervousness before you even take your new dog home. Ensure that the whole family meets the dog at the rescue centre and spends some quality time getting to know him. Try to visit more than once as this can really help your new dog feel more secure when home time arrives. He needs only one consistent aspect to his life in order to lower the threshold for becoming stressed, nervous or fearful: if he can recognize a family member and associate them with positive emotions, this will really help him to retain some confidence when coming into a strange situation. When bringing him home, try to make the car journey as stress-free as possible by making certain that your car has a dedicated area for your dog where he

will feel safe and secure. In an ideal world you will have a crate or dog guard separating the dog area so that he can comfortably settle down without having to be tied; if you haven't got one, try to borrow one. Put a waterproof car cover on the floor, because many dogs are travel sick, especially during the first journey to their new home. If you don't have a crate or dog guard, you can use a dog car harness to ensure that he is safe, although this still allows for some freedom. When you arrive home there are several steps you can take to help a nervous dog remain calm and relaxed.

Practical Guidelines: Management of the Nervous Dog at Homecoming

- Ensure that the whole household remains as calm and relaxed as possible and stop other family members from rushing over or overwhelming the dog (keep voices soft and neutral and ensure that children are calm and quiet).
- Have a handful of treats to lure him inside, and take your time; try not to pull or drag him but instead take small steps and use rewards encouragingly for each step forward.
- Guide him on a lead to the food and water station and offer him a drink (he is likely to be thirsty after the car journey - stressed dogs often pant heavily and need to cool down).
- Once he has had a drink it is important to show him the toilet area in the garden; drinking some water should help him to eliminate. Don't worry if he doesn't; just allow him to investigate the garden (on the lead, a long one if possible). Reward him softly if he goes to the toilet and offer a tasty treat (he may be too stressed to accept it but offering it may still activate posi-

tive emotions and dopamine production.

- Divide the house so that he can't access areas such as bedrooms where he can become trapped. Instead, set up a comfortable bed or crate covered with a blanket in a quiet area of the house. If you use a crate, leave the door open.
- At this stage take a break and leave him to sleep and become acclimatized until the next toilet time (after an hour or so). Whenever possible let him come to you rather than force him out of an area.
- Always have treats available to develop his trust and help him to feel more confident.
- Before you take him further than the garden, wait until he is showing trust and some confidence at home. If your dog is nervous, take him to a quiet area to begin with and keep walks short.

This crate has been covered over to act as a safe den area with the door open at all times.

THE OVER-ACTIVE DOG

It can be quite difficult to distinguish between over-active behaviour and normal playful behaviour, especially in young dogs. Very active dogs are not necessarily a problem and for many dogs high activity is an expression of happiness and well-being. Suppressing this behaviour may even cause dogs to become miserable and irritable, as well as leading to a multitude of other aberrant behaviours. However, extremely boisterous or over-active behaviour can be a problem in rescue dogs during the settling-in period. Interestingly, it can also occur once the dog grows in confidence, with dogs appearing to explode into over-active and juvenile displays. Generally this is the result of feeling dramatically better after weeks of suppression in a kennel. The first thing to realize is that this is normal behaviour for the way the dog is feeling; however, it's often difficult to cope with and can be reduced with patience, understanding and instruction.

Practical Guidelines: Management of the Over-Active Dog
- Put the brain and body to work: set a suitable physical and mental exercise routine. Avoid flooding the dog with fearful stimuli but ensure that you challenge him by taking him on at least two walks a day.
- Remember that mental exercise is equally as important as physical exercise. Begin conducting short (ten to fifteen minutes) and fun training sessions using positive reinforcement

DAY	DAILY POINT PLAN	DESIRED OUTCOME
0	• Prepare the home. Position vital equipment ready for homecoming • Ensure food and water bowl is positioned where it can be easily accessed at all times (water) • Ensure the bed is situated in a quiet area where the dog can rest without being disturbed	• You are confident and ready for the dog arriving home and the dog has everything he needs • Enables dog to access food and water whenever he needs, catering for his core needs (maintenance behaviours) • Helps the dog to feel safe and relaxed – aiding quality sleep (another core need/maintenance behaviour)
1	• Begin house-training routine even if the dog has a history of being fully toilet-trained (show garden on lead to begin with) • Hold off on cat introductions • Take on brief walk in quiet area only/garden play if fearful and unsure • Allow dog to sleep and rest as much as he wants without being disturbed	• Helps the dog to understand where he is supposed to go to the toilet and reduces stress for everybody by actively taking control rather than waiting for it to go wrong! • Allows dog and cat to settle and become aware of each other (scent) until stress of coming home/change of environment has reduced • Helps to introduce the location but prevents the dog from becoming overwhelmed or learning a fearful association with going outside/walking on lead • Will help him to gain required sleep and process the new information he is taking in. He may be tired from the kennel and this new change may cause him to need more rest than usual – allowing him to do this will help him to feel relaxed and secure and will support positive emotions
2	• Continue house-training • Add piece of cat's bedding to dog bed • Continue to take on quiet walks	• Reinforces desired behaviour • Enables dog to become familiar with the cat scent • Helps dog to become accustoned to the environment
3	• First cat introduction Start gradual introductions – make sure both animals have been fed and bring them into a room together, ensure the dog is on lead, cat in higher area (window ledge) and keep the dog at the furthest distance possible	At this stage hopefully both animals will be aware of their presence and gradual phase introductions help to prevent chase scenarios from occurring; prevents animals and owners become stressed

	Retain focus of the dog on handler by 'watch me' command (*see* Chapter 12) and reward calm, quiet behaviour (use high value treats throughout). Ensure the cat can have ability to run away but try to keep her calm by stroking/feeding in this area. End introduction one at this stage • Begin leaving for short periods alone while owners still in the house • If confident begin progression on walk/meet new people and new dogs (build gradually/do not overwhelm)	 • Helps the dog to become accustomed gradually to being left alone • Ensures that the dog is not overwhelmed by too much too soon but also means that he can start to socialize and learn that his new environment is not frightening

Having a plan to guide you through the first few days can be really helpful to reinforce the important parts of the settling-in period.

throughout. Introduce clicker training if suitable.

• Don't be afraid to allow your dog time to run off his energy. Let him go into the garden and have a 'crazy five minutes' running around.

• Try not to punish exuberant behaviour. This will make him increasingly wound up and tense; be direct and ensure that you give your dog clear commands to tell him what you want him to do. Stay consistent: avoiding punish-

This dog is jumping up through excitement, a common act if you are going to play with your dog on the ground!

ment doesn't mean you are a push-over; stay in control by directing and shaping your dog's behaviour.

- If he becomes so excited that he starts to jump up, bark loudly, or mouth your hand or other delicate objects, give him a job to do and reward him if he attempts it. You can also distract him by offering him a new toy or chew. This will help him to concentrate and take his mind off its chaotic path. Even a couple of seconds sitting and regaining focus can achieve this (*see* mat training in Chapter 5).

- Ensure he has plenty of chews and toys to mouth and release tension and energy.

- Relaxation and calm training can be extremely effective in such cases (*see* Chapter 5).

RETURNING YOUR RESCUE DOG: A LAST RESORT

Returning your dog to the rehoming centre should be the very last option because there is so much you can do to tackle numerous problems, many of which may be temporary. As soon as you begin to have problems with your rescue dog's behaviour, check that there are no health concerns. After this, it is imperative that you contact the rehoming centre. Many owners wait far too long before contacting the people who may be able to help them the most. The faster you act, the more effective training and modification can be. The rehoming centre will be able to advise you of any behaviourists or trainers that might be able to help you.

If the problem behaviour is serious, for example your dog has become very aggressive, you need to consider what this behaviour means for your family and your circumstances. The following questions should help you to make a decision at this traumatic and upsetting time.

- Can you manage the problem behaviour without family or friends being in danger?
- Are children involved? If so, fast action will be needed and returning the dog is often the safest option, even though it will cause him a degree of stress.
- Are you and your family still willing to work with the dog? It is important that each member is in agreement of this.
- Have you become fearful of the dog? Your fear may be contributing to the concern.
- Is the dog otherwise happy and content in your home and with your lifestyle? If he is unhappy and you have discovered that your lifestyle is not conducive to his welfare, it is important to consider this.

7 GENETIC INHERITANCE

It's well-documented that certain breeds are inclined to display particular behaviours more frequently than others: the border collie's herding drive and the foxhound's desire to track and follow scents are examples. Although it is absolutely possible to modify some innate behaviours with training and socialization, this often becomes increasingly difficult as dogs mature. My advice at this stage is to cast aside the idea that you can 'stop behaviour' completely; replace that idea with the vision of shaping and in some cases redirecting behaviour into something else. The questionable nature of dominance hierarchies existing between dogs and owners in the way that was once classically believed adds another complication to problems that are often perceived to be only 'skin deep'. The first part of this chapter aims to throw light on problematic 'traits' and consequent behaviours and to look from every angle at how to start the change. The second part examines so-called 'dominant' behaviours and investigates an alternative view of some real-life examples.

Even crossbreed dogs retain traits specific to their breeding.

Eye, Stalk, Chase

When problem behaviours occur as an expression of the dog's genes they can be particularly challenging to manage and modify. This is due to the 'weight' with which particular behaviours are rooted in the dog's make-up and evolutionary past. The physiological structure of the dog has great bearing on an overwhelming number of behaviours. For example, dogs have evolved as a predatory species; they are hunters, and therefore the prominent characteristics that facilitate this quality are going to reappear in everyday life, particularly when a corresponding stimulus is presented. The interesting thing is that humans have taken this process a step further and have overtly selected dogs for specific characteristics and bred them together to produce a group of dogs with superior abilities to carry out certain functions. This has enabled certain dogs to learn specific actions with greater ease, which predisposes them to behave in a particular manner more frequently. This can cause certain actions to become habitual and even 'second nature'.

The importance of this is simple: if you can understand where these 'natural' behaviours come from and how they are expressed in everyday life, you have a much greater chance of managing, controlling and even modifying them. According to Raymond and Lorna Coppinger (*see* Further Reading, page 189), the basic canine predatory behaviours consist of seven steps: orient, eye, stalk, chase, grab-bite, kill-bite, dissect. Interestingly, although as 'predators' all dogs are capable of following this sequence irrespective of size, physical make-up and breed, certain types of dogs have had their drive to perform parts of the sequence dampened down. This is why gundogs such as springer spaniels, labradors and retrievers can be successfully trained to perform select parts of the prey sequence and learn to flush, fetch and return game without inflicting damage. Other non-gun breed dogs instinctively find such behaviour much more difficult to perform.

The dog's predatory ancestors evolved through natural and artificial selection over thousands of years to become what we see today. Because of this predatory history, the domestic dog's ancestors inherited senses that facilitated their ability to hunt. While humans developed larger brains that enabled them to develop weapons and techniques to bring down larger prey, dogs were passing on genes responsible for an acute sense of smell and hearing, and social and co-operative abilities. This enabled them not only to work effectively and successfully with other members of their own species but also, quite amazingly, to develop the skills that were to play an important part in our own history.

MORE THAN SKIN-DEEP PROBLEMS

So what does this all mean and how does it affect you? Well, put simply, there are certain traits that can cause owners particular concern, often because they are at odds with the human environment. Ironically, it is worth noting that these 'problem' behaviours are in many cases desirable traits that have been favoured by humans. In fact, dogs that show an increased ability to display and learn these particular actions have been intentionally selected so that these characteristics become part of their 'breed' standard. Every dog's behaviour is an expression of what is within them, with

DOGS IN THE PAST AND THE PRESENT

Domestication reduces genetic variability, enabling specific traits to become more prominent and occur more frequently. The prehistoric dog became involved in this process tens of thousands of years ago, and the dog's acute senses would have been as beneficial to prehistoric man as they continue to be to humans today. Certain dog breeds appear to learn particular behaviour displays with greater ease than others; domestication has probably played a very influential role in this process.

Researchers have hypothesized that the dog evolved into the animal we see today by taking advantage of the ecological niches available to it. For example, scavenging around camps for the remains of human hunting, rather than hunting prey for themselves, would have required less energy and potentially have been less dangerous and more stable. At the same time it would be naïve to exclude the possibility that our human ancestors took advantage of the dog's natural and superior sensory abilities. A dog's acute sense of smell and hearing enables it to detect and then alert people to predators or prey – a useful trait for both prehistoric man and many of us today. The problem is, however, that the domestic dog's innate behaviours can very easily become at odds with their owners, especially if the owners are unaware, unprepared or unable to cater for these needs and drives. The results of this can be devastating. Although humans have had a vital part to play in producing the dogs we have come to know and love, they still as a species remain in part unnatural and awkward bystanders in houses all over the world.

The collie on the right is lying with belly close to the ground as his play friend bounces towards him; typical collie 'herding' behaviour.

their environment and learning experience thrown into the mix. Problematic behaviour is an expression of a multitude of factors. It is also valuable to remember that in working environments or homes where these traits are harnessed, focused and modified, these behaviours may not be problematic at all! This will be important in helping you to manage concerns such as the following.

- Extreme watchfulness and reluctance to break focus on external stimuli, particularly towards other animals or any moving stimulus (known as to high orient or eye).
- Many pastoral breeds, such as border collies and German shepherds, as well as sight hounds, such as greyhounds and lurcher types, can be problematic when out on walks and are difficult to keep focused. This is often a prelude to chasing behaviour, which can be a real hazard for other animals and people as well as the dogs themselves.
- Chasing and herding – owners who describe their dog as 'chasing everything that moves' may have considerable problems, particularly outside their home environment. Owners of both scent and sight hounds, lurchers, terriers, collies and some gundogs such as springer spaniels and weimaraners may have particular trouble curbing these drives.

- High territorial predisposition and suspicion of people – it's a natural behaviour for dogs to defend themselves, their home and their family if threatened. The problem arises, however, when this drive manifests itself in everyday life over threats that are of no real concern. Delivery service people, passers-by and, of course, the poor postal workers regularly and unwittingly fall into this category. Dogs used and bred for guarding purposes can learn to be suspicious of strangers, and owners must take care to ensure this learning doesn't become habitual; strict management is needed to tackle these concerns.
- High 'end' chain predatory drive – while out on walks, many dogs delight in chasing small animals such as rabbits and squirrels, and birds such as swans, geese and ducks. Some simply enjoy the chase and never get close enough to make the grab. However, those who

This German shepherd is an example of a pure-breed dog that has been selected over generations for specific traits.

Dogs don't have to be of guarding breed heritage to display these behaviours.

see, chase, grab and kill can be a completely different problem. If this behaviour includes livestock and even domestic pets, both you and your dog could be in serious trouble. It's not uncommon to hear of dogs being shot by farmers for worrying their livestock and if this predation covers family cats or even small dogs the problem can be equally serious.

CALMING THE DRIVE: CONTROLLING THE NATURAL DOG

Problem behaviour that relates to the dog's genetic make-up can be difficult to cope with. This is predominantly because these behaviours are easier for the dog to carry out when the stimulus to activate them is presented, and these are rife in daily life. So far I have discussed the importance that the learning and environmental components have on the dog, and at this stage they must be emphasized once again. When faced with any one of these problems, stopping the behaviour with harsh handling and punishment is likely to lead to mere suppression or redirection rather than tackle the cause. This is because this specific cause is rooted in the very being of the individual. Effectively tackling these problems, therefore, requires an intelligent sidestep into the contributing factors. You do, however, need to take charge of the situation and intervene and take precautions so that everybody concerned is kept safe. The following plan gives you practical tips on how to tackle behaviour resulting from the expression of the dog's genetic potential. I will then look at how to lower the intensity of these actions by specifically catering for these dogs and by harnessing their natural abilities to give them an outlet for this potential.

Harnessing the Natural Dog

Exercise is vitally important for dogs, but specific types enjoy particular activities

---

STARTING THE CHANGE

Before we look at the deepest level of shaping and tackling problem behaviour, I want to share with you the bare bones of my 'action plan' design. In order to manage and modify any undesirable behaviour effectively, you need to approach the issue with an analytical eye and without preconceptions. Using the mental image of 'shaping' rather than 'changing' behaviour is an important key to achieving your goals. This means that you will realize that you are getting somewhere when you see even a small part of what you want, rather than feeling defeated because your dog has not managed the whole behaviour in one go.

The key questions to ask about any behaviour that concerns you are: What does the behaviour consist of? When and where does the dog behave in this manner? These questions will help to identify the causes of the behaviour. Take note of your dog's behaviour right from the start, especially any actions that seems abnormal, or which interfere with your daily life and routine. Even small details can be very important in developing a picture of what is going on. Once you have the answers to these questions, you can ask the question 'Why?'

My action plans focus on three areas, abbreviated as PPMRR.

1. Prevent Practice (stop your dog practising the behaviour).
2. Manage (control the issues).
3. Retrain and Reinforce (counter-condition the behaviour).

PROBLEM BEHAVIOUR	MANAGEMENT AND SHAPING TIPS
High distraction due to high watchfulness	• Begin retraining the basics: ensuring your dog learns to respond to commands firs time (use lots of positive reinforcement; clicker if suitable) • Teach focusing command ('watch me' *see* Chapter 12), start training in quiet areas such as the garden • Conduct regular brief training extra to usual walks working on gaining focus and control (on lead to start) • Start increasing intensity of interactions (if busy park is the greatest distraction choose a quieter location with fewer people and walk closer to one if your dog remains calm and focused on you) • Practise the desirable response a couple of times then finish
Herding and chasing	• Breaking the herding cycle is vital if the behaviour is getting out of hand • Use distraction and paired reward when your dog stops the behaviour (use of whistle; reward on recall can be very useful to break this cycle) • Remember you will have to pair the whistle sound to reinforcement before beginning • Teach and reinforce recall, fetch and even basic tricks (sit, paw and down) to help automatically shape herding to other actions • Look for start of the chase; when stalking, lowering of body and intent watching begins, break this cycle and ask your dog to do something else • Practise this 'break and new response' routine to teach an alternative response • Use toys to direct this energy and keep the dog using his brain • Convert the drive rather than stop it; this helps to avoid frustration building • Keep practising and increase the intensity of interactions as the dog improves
Territorial tendencies	• Keep everybody safe (don't allow your dog to freely run to the danger areas such as the garden gate) • Turn pacing into actions making sure you keep an eye on stress, tension or concern building. For lesser cases retraining a new response will help teach the dog there is no need to guard their area; for others a more extensive plan may be needed • Change association; it's vital to teach that the presence of passers-by and visitors are no reason to be concerned: reward calm and confident behaviour • *See* Chapter nine for a deeper insight into what to do if the behaviour becomes aggressive

High predatory drive	• Ensure your dog is under lead control in areas where livestock and potential prey animals are in high numbers (muzzle training may be needed; *see* Chapter 9) • Retrain recall – vital in breaking the drive. Long lines can be useful to start retraining the recall and preventing your dog from running off while still having control • This drive can be very strong so care must be taken and very gentle desensitization starting gradually at a faraway distance; teaching the dog that these stimuli are not to be chased.

Practical management and shaping tips to help tackle genetic expression responsible for problem behaviours.

more than others. Finding ways of using the brain and body of these individuals and harnessing their potential and natural energy is vitally important in modifying problem behaviour and preventing it recurring. Standard exercise opportunities such as providing a well-balanced and varied external environment can be challenging for owners with dogs that tend to chase or prey on anything that moves. There are, however, additional places and activities you can become involved in that can help to focus these drives. Organized group walks can pro-

Agility can test dogs mentally and physically. These two are enjoying playing around this tunnel.

vide excellent opportunities for your dogs to play, but training and socialization classes can also be a great way to teach your dog how to focus in a controlled environment. Further obedience training and heelwork to music can be a fantastic tool for mentally exercising dogs, and agility and trail work can provide physical action for dogs with high energy. The key is to focus the problem dog's energy onto a favourable action and behaviour rather than simply allow him to practise the undesirable actions or try unsuccessfully to stop them. Stopping can lead to suppression and recovery (often coming back more extreme). Conversion, retraining and reinforcement direct the behaviour that results from specific motivating factors into different response pathways, and thus modify the behaviour that you see.

DOMINANCE PROBLEM BEHAVIOUR

Problem dogs are frequently branded as dominant in order to explain numerous behavioural discrepancies, particularly disobedience and aggression. A dominance hierarchy classically refers to the organization of a group of animals of the same species, and concerns the control and circulation of resources within a territory. Higher-ranking individuals gain control through a dominance contest that gives them the right to obtain resources such as food and mating rights above other members of the group. This in turn enables them to achieve reproductive superiority.

The word dominance, and in particular the phrase 'dominant dog', divides opinion among behaviourists, trainers and owners. What exactly is the principle of a dominance hierarchy existing between dogs and humans? Treatment based on dominance often involves training aimed at lowering the dog's status, sometimes using methods intended to invoke submission and fear. If the dog's behaviour isn't based on domineering motivations, attempts to reduce his status may not only be unnecessary and confusing for the dog, but can also be detrimental to the overall relationship, especially if treatment involves the latter approach. If you think it's just a difference in terminology, think again, because this terminology often has a direct impact on the treatment the dog receives. When people believe that their dog is challenging their status, they are often very quick to do all they can to reduce him to a submissive role. At its mildest, attempts to reduce 'dominance' are limited to obedience and control – for example, training your dog to walk through a door behind you rather than pulling you through it (definitely a desirable thing to learn!). In more extreme cases the dominant dog may be 'forced' to be submissive and subservient through the use of punishment, despite the possibility that his behaviour may not be motivated by status at all.

One of the main problems I come across on a daily basis relates to owners locked in battle with their dogs as they attempt to curb what are perceived as domineering actions. Short-term wins are often superseded by long-term failure, with problem behaviour frequently recurring and regularly becoming more severe. These owners are left feeling weak, angry and frustrated; actions that originated in a desire to keep control over the relationship, end as uncontrollable outbursts that the dog has great difficulty in understanding. The dogs involved can be equally confused, defensive, suspicious, and often fearful of the next encounter,

DOMINANCE IN THE PAST, PRESENT AND FUTURE

For thousands of years dogs have been involved in the process of domestication. This process has resulted in the domestic dog's variety in appearance, smaller brain size and varying physiological characteristics. Dog training methods, particularly the principles of dominance reduction techniques, are regularly based upon the study of wolves. Early studies focused on wolves in captivity that weren't necessarily related but had been brought together from various sources and kept together for many years. Thus these findings are likely to distort the truth of a real wolf pack, in which dominance contests are not as common as once believed. The domestic dog is genetically very similar to the grey wolf, but they are in fact quite different. Domestication has been documented as causing developmental delay, resulting in juvenile traits at maturity known as neotony. Since tameness and aggression are regulated by hormones, selecting for tameness and against aggression could bring about a change to the physiological traits associated with domestication and neotony.

Neotony (developmental delay seen in domestic dogs) suggests that dogs are mentally at the stage of the adolescent wolf or the wolf cub, and are not psychologically prepared to take on the responsibilities of a pack. Therefore the idea that they need guidance, training and reinforcement rather than aggressive leadership becomes more appropriate and realistic.

Finally, a dominance hierarchy typically refers to a group of animals of the same species. Therefore it's important to question the impact this factor must have on the reality of a hierarchy consisting of two distinct species. To suggest that dogs view humans simply as 'other dogs' seems a complete over-simplification. Our 'juvenile wolf', the dog, who lacks the maturity to take responsibility and leadership of the pack, is unlikely to regard humans as other dogs; he certainly can't understand us in the same way, and he has a lower need to control resources than the free-ranging individuals of a wolf pack. All this suggests that some, if not all, so-called 'dominant behaviour' is actually the result of another psychological process.

This crossbreed puppy has the piebald colouring and floppy ears caused by domestication.

PERCEIVED TO BE DOMINANT BEHAVIOUR	ALTERNATIVE MOTIVATION AND CAUSE
Jumping up	• Greeting behaviour reflecting attention and care seeking behaviour • Control movement of owner through fear of consequences (often past learning)
Walking through doors first/ pushing past owners	• Eagerness to go somewhere/get to the other side. • Dogs with fear relating to the outside may rush round corners to investigate if threats are located around them. This has nothing to do with dominance
Try to sit on owners/gaining proximity and putting paws on you	• Affection • Play and excitement • Attention • Lack of security (getting close to owners and visitors can be a way to feel more secure); commonly seen in dogs with insecure attachment status • Control (triggered by fear)
Sitting on sofas/increasing height	• Lack of confidence can cause dogs to seek higher positions so that they have clearer views; control over the situation and are higher to defend themselves
Resource-guarding and possessiveness	• Insecurity around these items (potentially due to a lack of resources in the past) • Learnt response that something negative will happen when owners are close to resources held (commonly through past events such as being struck for not letting go of food/toys which can teach them to be defensive)
Staring or making prolonged eye contact	• Fear • Insecurity • Frozen watching – commonly seen among very fearful dogs anticipating human movement through learning association with negative events
Growling or barking	• Fear • Distress
Mouthing	• Stress • Control (through learning and initial fear)
Showing reluctance to be handled	• Fear • Uncertainty • Pain • Learning (of negative emotions and association)

Many commonly-perceived problem behaviours are likely by-products of alternative motivating factors.

which regularly disrupts daily life together. I regularly see communication break down and relationships implode.

So Is Your Dog Really Trying To Dominate You?

The answer to this question is far from simple, but I consistently find that using confrontation and harsh methods to reduce the dominance of your dog is not conducive to successfully tackling problem behaviour. I am uncomfortable with the concept of the dominant dog fuelling so many behaviour problems, because many so-called 'dominant' actions could be caused by other factors, in particular by a dog's insecurity and fear. Moreover, these emotions will increase in intensity when threatened with further conflict and stress. It is therefore possible that an animal under stress, confused and with a disruption in his core needs, might demonstrate what was classically known as 'dominant' behaviour, which in reality is a by-product of his emotional state.

Dogs are complex mammals with a survival drive not unlike our own. They have the ability to feel emotions, including fear, and to recognize when they need to display threatening behaviours. In view of this, you should be sympathetic to their response to perceived threats, and make an effort to understand when they are feeling this way. If you substitute the word 'survival' for the adjective 'dominant', as in 'survival behaviour', then you can make the important discovery that there is something going wrong with a relationship in which a dog is showing any 'survival behaviour'. We can then ask what could be wrong rather than simply ascribe these actions to an inborn desire to be dominant. Behaviour displays may well be the result of varying influences that, as you have already seen, carry so much weight in the actions you see.

Rules, control and obedience aren't only desirable in canine and human relationships, they are absolutely necessary for successful living. This can be achieved by guidance, training and reinforcement; by using the positive kind you can maintain and build the trust and security that are essential in all relationships. Many problem behaviours that are often attributed to status can in fact be caused by a multitude of other factors. Branding your dog as a dominant individual may not be just, useful and, most importantly, conducive to successfully tackling the issues you are having.

The following three case studies aim to reveal how problem behaviour that is regularly put down to domineering motivation can be caused by alternative factors.

CASE STUDY: RHONA

Rhona is a two-year-old female German shepherd that has shown aggression towards her owner for the first time. The aggressive episode occurred when her owner pinned her to the ground by force. This treatment was inflicted upon Rhona for displaying mouthing behaviour and hurting her owner's hand. Rhona's owners perceived this behaviour as the start of a dominance contest and inflicted punishing actions to try to reduce Rhona's status.

There are two significant problems to this line of thinking which need to be examined:

1. Was Rhona's original 'problem behaviour' the result of dominating motivation? (If not, the cause of the concern has not been taken into consideration.)

2. Is Rhona capable of understanding why she has been punished, so that she can and will know not to do it again? (If not, this action may at best cause short-term suppression of behaviour and at worst create more severe displays, unpredictability and distrust.)

I hope this helps you to see what a vitally important topic this is and encourages you to question the motive of your dog's behaviour in more detail. If so-called dominant behaviours are in fact the result of a different psychological process and different motivation, then surely this puts dominance reducing treatment into doubt in all cases?

Mouthing can be caused by a range of motivational factors. This dog is mouthing in play; it's not a desirable trait.

CASE STUDY: WILBER

Wilber is a two-year-old neutered male labrador whose owner contacted me because he had just bitten her while she was sitting on the sofa stroking him. Wilber's history was tragic: he had been found as a stray and rehomed by the Dogs Trust as an eight-month-old puppy and was very affectionate but thin and in poor condition. He had never shown any negative displays or aggression at any stage of rehoming or during assessment. When Wilber arrived home his owners (male and female) stuck to a dominance reduction plan, using aggression, punishment and force if he displayed any concerning behaviour. Concerning behaviour covered anything from jumping up and pulling on the lead to bouts of excitement and aggression. At the beginning of the second day Wilber growled when his male owner approached his food bowl while he was eating. His owner used severe punishing actions to 'treat' the concern in an attempt to reduce his status. He did not take into consideration that hunger, previous food deprivation and insecurity were more likely to have fuelled the display. Wilber was thin, confused and had yet to settle in his new home; this treatment affected him so severely that it was a year before he could again eat confidently from his food bowl in this area. At the same point in time Wilber took to sitting on sofa areas in the corners of rooms and taking up defensive positioning, displaying growling, and snapping when people attempted to drag him off. The sofas became resources for Wilber to feel safe. A year later the bite incident occurred and at this stage Wilber would nip, snap and bite his owners at various times such as when they leant over to pick up the television remote, stroked him while asleep, and even walked past him. Wilber continued to be affectionate but became increasingly insecure, and affection displays tilted into insecurity in desperate efforts to appease his owners.

When I came to visit Wilber and his family I was deeply saddened to hear the position they were now in: Wilber had been booked into the vet's to be euthanased. Unravelling the past revealed that Wilber's displays appeared to be linked more to fear and insecurity, and even hunger in the beginning. The treatment he received not only taught him to be defensive, insecure and afraid, but also inconsistent in his emotional reactions to any action he regarded as a potential threat (ambivalent attachment). I started Wilber's owners on a plan of action not only to stop the practice of the behaviour by teaching him to target and sit on the floor (on comfortable bedding, mats and blankets) and avoid the sofa areas, but also to build his security, confidence and attachment. One week later the plan was already working and proved to be a great success. Wilber needed rules, guidance and training; but in this case his owners' wrong decision to use aggression in order to dominate him very nearly cost Wilber his life.

Dogs can be motivated to sit on the sofa for many reasons; sometimes a lack of confidence can spur this behaviour.

CASE STUDY: TINNY

Tinny is a ten-year-old Jack Russell who had been displaying aggressive behaviour since adolescence. Aggression started when Tinny didn't want to do something she was asked. Her owner used aggressive actions in response to these displays in order to lower her status but the behaviour became increasingly severe over the years. Tinny suffered from regular bouts of stress and took to hiding under furniture or jumping and backing into corners of chairs when her owner approached. She regularly snapped and bit her owner's hands when attempts were made to pull her off and this cycle kept getting progressively worse. When I went to visit Tinny she appeared to be a sweet, affectionate dog but it was clear that she had become used to reacting on a path of acute stress. Tinny was taught from a young age that close contact at times of concern would result in negative events occurring. This taught her to value space and height highly as these areas would keep her in an advantageous position. The key to unravelling this concern was firstly to prevent Tinny from practising and acting on this emotion and then retraining her response. When dogs have been practising behaviour for long periods of time the condition can become habitual and very much part of their repertoire. The key is to teach these individuals a new way of being, while ensuring that the surrounding environment lowers stress wherever possible. Tinny's plan reflected this and worked at teaching her that her owners were no longer going to harm her. She was also retrained to act on command and do the necessary actions needed in everyday life.

It's important that your dog listens to you and behaves in the way you need them to do; however, the best relationships for all concerned are based on trust and respect through understanding.

8 FEAR AND DISTRESS

Fear plagues many dogs and their owners. These emotions can result in behaviour displays ranging from the inconvenient right through to the plain dangerous. The trouble is that it can be very difficult to understand fear as it affects another animal who is unable to talk and explain why they are afraid. In this chapter we shall investigate the psychology of the fearful dog and the practical implications of actions motivated by fear. Fear and distress are significant causes of some of the most troubling behavioural problems and are often very difficult to cope with. This chapter explores the practical side of tackling such concerns while helping you to get to grips with not only managing these problems but also modifying them.

WHAT IS FEAR?

Everyone knows what it feels like to be afraid. Fear can make you feel upset, out of control, frantic and even angry. Uncontrollable outbursts of emotion are commonplace as people attempt to control the situation, cope with it, or make the source of fear go away. The reasons for these varied responses differ as much as people's reactions to fear. The fact of the matter remains the same, however: when you are faced with a threatening stimulus, be it a loud bang from a car backfiring or a stranger approaching with a knife, it produces a physiological and psychological reaction. This 'reaction' is hardwired into all animals, including dogs, as an innate mechanism to help them survive.

There are many things that can cause your dog to become afraid; they may not even have to be faced with pain or a direct threat for a very similar reaction to take place (for example, separation distress).

Anxiety is a little more difficult to understand in dog psychology because it relates to stress caused by both impending and current events. Anxiety and distress are by-products of standard fear and often develop when the dog can't control the situation or follow the standard mechanism of escape, avoid or defend (when fight or flight are disabled, the stress and fear energy produces anxious behaviour). It's very difficult to conclude that dogs experience and process the fear emotion in the same way as humans because of our ethological (evolutionary), physiological and psychological differences. At a basic level humans and dogs share the same fear reaction and survival drive, but it's vital to remember that they do not share the same ability to process the meaning of these emotions.

This has significant bearing on how to examine behavioural problems and highlights the importance of being aware of anthropomorphism (attributing human emotions to animal behaviour) when tackling your dog's concerns. It is useful to sympathize with your dog's fear because this will help you to understand the concern rather than simply dismiss it. But it's important not to pour this emotion outwards onto your dog, because they will have difficulty understanding what it means and may inadvertantly contribute to the problem through misinterpretation. Put simply, tackle fear-related concerns with patience, kindness and understanding, but remember that dogs simply can't and don't think exactly like humans.

CAUSES OF FEAR

If fear means feeling threatened and having your survival put in potential jeopardy, it is vital to consider what stimuli can produce this reaction. Briefly, absolutely anything can cause a dog to show a fearful reaction! Your dog can learn to associate any object or situation with fear. This is most likely through the experience or anticipation of a negative stimulus such as pain or stress; among under-socialized individuals it is common for this response to be invoked by unfa-

miliar people, objects and environments as they have yet to be proven non-threatening. Remember that once this association has been learnt, a fearful response can occur when the dog is faced with a similar stimulus even if it poses no direct threat or is less intensive. The stress reaction is intertwined with fear: as we saw earlier, when dogs become frightened the stress response is activated.

Pain is one such 'fear-provoking stimulus'; as a sensory reflex it informs the brain that the body is in danger and therefore needs to act to regulate homeostasis. For example, a dog receives a bite from another, which activates the pain receptors on the skin. This message transfers to the brain, which processes it and tells the animal to act accordingly (the hypothalamic-pituitary-adrenal axis is activated and the 'fight or flight' mechanism commences). If the dog did not react internally and externally to the pain from this bite, homeostasis and indeed survival itself would be in jeopardy. There are certain situations and scenarios which tend to produce this reaction more than others, and knowing what to do to tackle fear is very important.

Dogs can show signs of fear towards many things. This dog is frightened of a stone statue representing a dog!

MORE THAN JUST FLIGHT OR FIGHT?

The 'flight or fight' concept is well documented and ingrained in human society; however, when fear strikes it can cause additional behavioural effects. Frightened dogs commonly show this emotion through frozen, stiff body language. They can also become restless, displaying displacement behaviours (normal behaviours carried out at odd times) such as self-grooming, lapping water and sniffing genitals. Calming signals are also commonly seen when dogs become fearful, and these can be early indicators that dogs are worried. Some dogs have even been known to faint, which although rare conveys how dramatic the effects of fear can be.

CLEO

I first met Cleo, a young female collie, huddled in the back of a kennel. Cleo had been rescued from Ireland with another dog, Mark, who was probably a relation and was blind. Although Mark was wary of people, his uncertainty was mild compared to Cleo's fear of people, which was both dramatic and extreme. She would freeze as soon as anyone approached, shake, tremble, display an array of calming signals and at times show complete shutdown of behaviours (tonic immobility). Both Cleo and Mark had lived in barrels in a rural area, although little else was known about their background. Introducing Cleo to prospective owners was very difficult as she was very avoidant. Care had to be taken to ensure she was not overwhelmed by interactions that would only confirm her fear. Interestingly, Cleo was able to make bonds and relate to people relatively quickly, conveying that she had social skills and was able to recognize

The springer spaniel on the left is displaying a tongue flick calming signal due to the chocolate collie's behaviour towards her.

humans as attachment figures. Cleo's concern was focused on those she didn't know and with whom she had not yet developed trust. In addition to this, Cleo's herding behaviour towards other dogs was high and when new people were introduced this intensified due to the increased stress she was experiencing. During an interaction with a prospective new owner and their dog, Cleo became increasingly intense, focused on herding, and showing fear and stress-related behaviour towards the new person. After only a short time this interaction proved too much for Cleo and she began to walk as if through heavy sand, her breathing increased and she collapsed for a few moments. It was a very strange sight and one that has stayed with me throughout my work.

It is very useful to remember that the most commonly known and recognized signs of fear, 'flight or fight', are in fact only part of the picture. The example of Cleo highlights that there are other mechanisms at work. Many of these are focused on communicating and defusing tension both physically and mentally. If your dog freezes when he is approached or when attempts are made to touch him, this should ring alarm bells in your mind.

FEAR CAUSING STIMULI	RESULTING PROBLEM BEHAVIOUR	HOW THIS AFFECTS YOU
Owner	• Reluctance to approach or join in with social interactions • Submissive urination • Inappropriate toileting behaviour • In severe cases stereotypical behaviour displays (spinning, wall-licking, tail-chasing) • Barking, growling and potentially aggressive behaviours presented	• Creates feelings of worry and concern for dog, owner and visitors • Extra cleaning • Potential embarrassment and even anger
People (visiting)	• Reluctance to approach or join in with social interactions • Submissive urination; inappropriate toileting behaviour • In severe cases stereotypical behaviour displays (spinning, wall-licking, tail-chasing) • Barking, growling and potentially aggressive behaviours presented towards visitor	• Creates feelings of worry and concern for dog, owner and visitors • Extra cleaning • Potential embarrassment and even anger especially if either party is put in a potentially harmful situation (aggression shown from dog or visitor) • May even prevent you from allowing visitors inside the house • Complaints may be made
People (outside)	• May present any of the behaviours above; intensifying as people get closer	• Makes walking difficult; potentially hazardous • Limits walks and areas you can go to
Other dogs	• Reluctance to walk outside; stress and nervousness while out; pulling in different directions and uneasiness often accompanies this behaviour • Defensive behaviour may be presented/becoming more extreme the closer the dog gets to another dog	• Makes walking in the outside world difficult • Pulling back on the lead near roads can be dangerous • Embarrassment and disappointment can be caused by these actions; the behaviour may cause you to keep your dog away from others completely which can lead to further frustration

	• Fear/defensive behaviour	• Potential injury for all concerned creating fear and nervousness for everyone concerned
Noise (fireworks etc)	• Can lead to extreme fear and stress • Barking behaviour may be presented; disrupted sleep potentially causing irritability • Reluctance to go out and potential toileting concerns • Stereotypical behaviour is a possibility	• Worry and concern • Potential for noise complaints. Further concerns may be presented through lack of security • Increased cleaning
Travel	• Extreme fear, stress and concern when faced with travelling. In severe cases just getting to the car can cause problems	• Makes travel very difficult; can even limit where you go

The variety of stimuli that can cause fear and the effect that these have on your daily life with your dog.

IDENTIFYING FEAR AND NERVOUSNESS

Having established what fear is, what can cause it and how it affects dogs, it is vital to be aware of the signals. Severe fear can be easily recognized, but having the skills to identify the smaller signs of your dog experiencing a fearful response is absolutely invaluable. This is particularly useful when you come to shape and modify your dog's behaviour. The more effective you can become at recognizing that your dog is becoming fearful, the more successful you will be at tackling the concern. The following signs of fear are worth keeping in mind throughout your daily life and interaction with your dog.

SIGNS OF FEAR

The Body

Characteristically a fearful dog may show a low body posture, with lowered head and tail. Many dogs appear to creep very low to the ground and some may even crawl with their stomach touching the floor. Their movements may appear rigid and purposeful, even frozen, with head and eyes focused on the fear-provoking stimulus. The dog's body may be shaking, trembling and tense, which relates to the stress mechanism and adrenaline production. They are likely to have sweaty paws and submissive urination; even defecation may be presented in severe cases. Another sign that relates to adrenaline production and is important to look out

This dog's low body posture is being caused by fear of being handled to put on her lead.

This dog is showing several signs of fear due to the hand approaching her.

for is raised hair over the top of the shoulders and along the spine.

Face and Ears

Dogs' eyes can be extremely expressive and give you a great deal of insight into the emotions they are feeling, especially when it comes to fear. I find dogs' eyes and expressions invaluable when working and living with them. A dog's eye movements, eye shape and direction of gaze, as well as how often eye contact is made and for how long, can tell me a great deal about the dog's state of mind. Frowning, facial furrows and expression lines are also revealing. Fascinatingly, this is due to the social evolution of their species with ours; their ability to read us effectively by our eye and body language is an invaluable trait for learning and working alongside humans. This is a core part of the success of our relationship throughout history. The easiest way to understand this is to experience it. When with your dog, watch for him 'checking in' (making eye contact); you may find it surprising how often this occurs.

Although dogs can understand some human vocals, they are experts at body language and look at our eyes in particular to gauge what is about to happen. Fearful dogs often have a wide-eyed expression and may show the sclera (whites of their eyes). They may be frozen in their watchfulness to assess the situation as effectively as possible; others may be reluctant to engage eye contact because it is too threatening for them and avoiding eye contact is a way to reduce this tension. A happy, confident and relaxed dog will make eye contact readily; he will 'check in' with his owners when needed but remain calm, and his other body language will mirror this. The fearful dog's pupils may be dilated to help him gain as much information as possible through vision to evaluate the situation. This is often accompanied by ridges around the face, and don't forget to look out for stress signs: panting heavily and holding the tongue rigidly out of the mouth (often wider at the bottom and maybe even curled, rolled or bent). The fearful dog may even have a 'sucking lemons' expression in his mouth, with a tight-lipped appearance. The ears are often clamped to the dog's head or held rigid with tension. The face of the fearful dog is very different and the opposite of the soft, round and relaxed expression of a happy, confident dog. A key part of recognizing fear is being able to recognize tension. Always look out for tension building, because tension is the most obvious and basic element of fear running through the fearful dog.

The Jack Russell on the right is displaying how fear and concern can be translated through the face and body.

This little collie is displaying a paw lift and a very uncertain expression while on the lead.

Full Body Shaking

Watch for full body shaking (as if shedding water). This can be caused by many things and is due to the release of adrenaline. It's the dog's way of shaking off tension and getting back to a normal homeostatic level. Full body shaking often occurs after even minor stress events. Conflicts with other dogs, human handling, noise – in fact anything that causes a change in the body's internal levels can cause this response. It's a positive action, revealing that your dog is trying to get back to normal and should be rewarded. Use vocal praise such as 'good shake' when it happens.

Tail

Fearful dogs often clamp their tails low, between and under their back legs to cover their genitals. Once again the fearful dog's tail is often ridged and tense.

The dog may be reluctant to move it and even if the tail does start to rise as the dog gains confidence, it often remains low and stiff when moved. Through the effects of adrenaline some dogs show raised hair over the base of their tail when afraid. In addition it is important to remember that the fearful dog may actually wag his tail and far from a sign that all is well, this can in fact be a calming signal. It is very likely that it will be rigid and wooden in appearance with smaller, hesitant circular motions rather than the large motion of the loosely wagging tail of a confident, happy dog. This highlights why it is really important to judge the dog by his whole body rather than just one area. Identifying these subtle signs can be really helpful in successfully recognizing that your dog is fearful and when you need to act.

Legs
Watch out for paw lifts and movement of the front feet when the dog is standing or sitting still. Uneasiness, unsettled movement and frantic behaviour often accompany these signs. They can be calming signals if they are directed towards the cause of fear and may be displacement behaviours if self-directed. Once again slow movement and a rigid pace is likely to accompany the moving limbs of the fearful dog. If the dog is bound by a restraint such as a lead, held by hand, or confined or backed into a smaller area,

the fear behaviour and signs are likely to be more extreme. This is simply because the flight option is disabled, putting greater pressure on the other options available to the dog.

BEHAVIOURAL PROBLEMS ASSOCIATED WITH FEAR

Fearful and chronically distressed dogs can be very difficult to live with. Fearful, phobic and distressed dogs can be noisy, destructive, worrying and often, causing most concern, aggressive. This makes perfect sense if you consider that for the frightened dog aggression is a natural response to guard themselves against threatening stimuli, especially if they have no other option (they can't flee and other signals are having no effect). The reason dogs do this is very simple: it fundamentally helps them to survive. This survival drive is a powerful force and may help you to understand why even the most good-natured dogs can show aggressive behaviours if they are put in a

The drawing shows the tilted position fearful dogs often adopt when worried.

This drawing shows the same dog in a standard upright position.

threatening situation. The speed at which a dog reaches an aggression response depends on several factors including health, development, learning, environment and experience.

Things get a little more complicated when you consider that the dog is also capable of developing negative associations with threatening stimuli. In these situations dogs can display fearful or even aggressive behaviour when exposed to the remembered stimuli or one that is similar even if less intensive. If the dog is prevented from carrying out his first choice of actions you may also be faced with frustration, redirection and even stereotypical actions. These behaviours can be additional problems. There are a range of behaviours resulting from fear that are more inconvenient than anything else, but they must still be addressed as they can develop into further problems and become more extreme; submissive urination is one such issue. It is also always important to remember that a fearful dog is unlikely to be happy. Acute and chronic stress plagues many fearful dogs, which is a very worrying place to be.

The next chapter is dedicated to aggression because this can be a complicated concern needing substantial explanation. At this stage I want to show you how to cope with fearful reactions and how to help your dog overcome them. As I have said, dogs can become fearful of absolutely anything; however, throughout my work I come across two main reasons that commonly evoke this response: fear of people and fear of other dogs. The more specific fears relating to changes in environment will be reviewed in Chapters 10 and 11 (problems within and outside the home), but for now I want to take you on a journey

Even people at a distance can cause dogs to become fearful.

to discover how to swap fear for confidence.

FEAR OF PEOPLE

Dogs that are fearful of people have a very tough time living in the modern world, principally because it is full of humans! This is one of the occasions when it can be really useful to try to empathize with your dog in order to understand how terrifying the world must be for him. If the fear extends to those cohabiting with the dog, it adds another dimension to the concern because everyday life can be very difficult. It should be tackled as early as possible because, like so many other fears, the more practised the dog becomes at being

SUBMISSIVE URINATION

This is an upsetting and awkward experience due to the obvious stress and upset displayed by such dogs. Submissive urination occurs much more frequently amongst puppies and younger dogs, but fearful adults also regularly suffer. The constant cleaning necessary to manage the mishaps in the house is another significant problem resulting from these actions. Submissive urination is often accompanied by fearful signs such as ears laid back, tail tucked under, lowered body and potential cowering, while avoiding eye contact. These dogs may also roll over to reveal the stomach and show appeasement behaviour. Triggers for this behaviour are often related to human gestures, sounds or even facial expressions that are perceived by the dog as frightening and threatening. Gestures such as leaning over, touching the top of the head, cuddling and even approaching can be enough to evoke this response. These gestures may appear totally unthreatening to many dogs but those who are fearful and lack confidence can very easily become concerned. Harsh, loud and aggressive vocals are other causes of this concern. The reason behind it may relate to general sensitivity or previous experience such as harsh handling, pain and punishment, as well as lack of socialization. Inadequate socialization to people or other dogs and animals can very easily create a fearful response. This may not be due to negative associations through learning but because these stimuli are unknown and as yet unsafe. This is an important factor to remember all through this chapter because it explains why gradual exposure to frightening stimuli is so important.

afraid and even rewarded for avoiding this fear, the deeper the association becomes. Fear of people can be further divided into three sections: fear of owners, fear of visitors, and fear of strangers.

Where Does Fear Come From?
There are two principle factors that present as causes for dogs to be afraid of people:

1. People are frightening because they are associated with negative experiences and events.
2. People are seen as non-safe in varying degrees, and in some cases as almost 'alien', through lack of socialization.

While out on walks, it's sometimes impossible to avoid people and other dogs. These three are meeting for the first time but they are also coming into contact with the new dogs' owners.

CASE STUDY: MARLEY

Dogs that have lacked adequate socialization to humans can be extremely and chronically fearful individuals. Marley, a young chocolate labrador, was such a dog. He was found raiding dustbins as a stray, rescued, and brought to a Dogs Trust rehoming centre in Newbury to start the process of finding a new home. It was here that staff noticed he was not an average stray. Marley was totally petrified of all people. He was completely avoidant and would not approach anyone; when attempts were made to put his lead on he would lie down, shake, close his eyes and panic. This behaviour didn't ease off after a few weeks as he got to know certain staff members, as is often the case with other fearful dogs, but continued month after month. Marley was consistently avoidant in all situations, inside and outside; the smaller the environment in which he found himself when people were present, the more he began to panic through his inability to stay at a 'safe' distance. Even watching and being kennelled with a confident and people-friendly dog did little to teach him a new response. Nobody could touch or stroke him and the stress and displacement signs presented when people were close to him were extreme.

It took over a year to teach Marley the most basic social skills and for him to be able to lean towards my hand while being stroked. This was an unbelievable step forward. Two specific details of Marley's case were relevant to dogs that have lacked socialization. Firstly, he was frightened of everyone; there was no pattern to his distrust. Secondly, he found it almost impossible to form any bond or relationship with any human and had absolutely no understanding of people.

CASE STUDY: PEPPER

Pepper was a young collie rescued from Ireland. Like Marley, she was very fearful of people but she was particularly fearful of men. Tragically, Pepper had burn scars around her neck, most probably due to the use of an electric shock collar. Although wary at first and generally suspicious of all people, Pepper was able to form bonds with several female staff members; however, her behaviour towards men was quite different. Over time she began to learn to trust certain male individuals but remained alert and fearful of unfamiliar men.

The primary difference between dogs that are fearful through negative experiences with people and those who have had very little or no experience of them lies in the bonding potential. If dogs miss out on socialization they find it extremely difficult to develop bonds with people because they have very little or no knowledge of how to act and what to do. They must play a game of social catch-up and learn that there is no reason to be afraid of the wide spectrum of human behaviours and gestures, which actually may mean something! The dog that has experienced a frightening or negative association with people is likely to be able to form close bonds with certain people but may continue to find particular individuals frightening because of these negative associations.

FEAR OF OTHER DOGS

Dogs are a social species and have a natural social disposition. Lack of early socialization (being taken from the mother at too young an age), under-habituation and experience are all factors that can impact this evolutionary inclination. Owners of dogs fearful of others can struggle inside and outside the home environment, particularly as these individuals are missing the natural interaction with their own species. This is not to say that humans don't make fantastic companions for dogs, but it's different. Dogs interact, play and socialize in a manner we can't entirely replicate, and in the large majority of cases canine interaction is helpful for relieving stress, learning and general happiness. Once again I would highlight the important role that fear has to play in aggression. It's also worth noting that lack of experience and negative experiences can emphasize and contribute to same-species, status-related concerns (commonly seen among males, less commonly among females). The important thing to take from this is that if you have a dog that shows fear towards others you need to act now.

The key to unravelling this fear will be discussed in the next section, but here I would like to introduce two vitally important points: firstly, don't flood the dog with what frightens him; and secondly, build positive experiences and associations at a lower level and move at your dog's pace.

HELPING THE FEARFUL DOG

Noise Fears and Phobias

Bonfire Night is a dreaded time for many pet owners. Similarly, gunfire, cars backfiring, and household appliances can cause extreme fear, sometimes phobic in nature. I have worked with many dogs suffering from these concerns; one female collie was so severely affected that she refused to leave the house for six months after fireworks night! Although such noises sound loud and startling to us, consider how they can sound to a dog's acute senses. Science tells us that dogs have the ability to hear much higher frequencies than humans, so it's not difficult to hypothesize that a car backfiring, a gunshot, the vacuum cleaner, and of course the dreaded fireworks are likely to be much greater fear-provoking stimuli. Coupled with the fact that dogs don't

There is tension between these three dogs. Well-socialized dogs learn how to pacify situations and defuse conflict, as Thelma (the black and tan dog on the left) is revealing. Fearful dogs can learn to be defensive and potentially aggressive.

understand the purpose of these noise occurrences, this produces a volatile mix. Why some dogs become concerned by such noise and others do not depends on various factors and is in part a mystery. I can speculate that sensitivity, general confidence level, past learning and experience are all-important factors. Helping your dog overcome these issues once again fits into the PPMRR action plan (prevent practice, manage, retrain and reinforce). I have developed a five point plan below to help you deal with noise concerns both inside and outside the home.

1. If your dog suffers from noise concerns it's important to lessen these stimuli wherever possible both internally (by training and changing the emotional reaction) and externally (by management when noise is occurring).
2. Prepare for louder noise by a gentle desensitization plan, working only at your dog's level. There are several 'noise CDs' available for this purpose, but you must introduce them gradually and follow the instructions. Similarly, if outside noise is the problem, start walking in quiet areas and gradually build intensity.
3. Counter condition your dog's emotions by giving him simple tasks to do and buckets of positive reinforcement. Do this indoors while the noise CD takes effect; outside, positively encourage and reinforce counter-commands such as the 'watch me' (see Chapter 12).
4. Mat training provides an additional method of counter-conditioning while providing and training your dog to target a safe place at times of concern.
5. On Bonfire Night, walk your dog before darkness falls to avoid being caught outside. Inside, ensure that he

has a variety of safe places to go; supplying him with an extra duvet to hide under may be useful. Turning the TV and radio up to help him concentrate on other noise can also be helpful.

TEACHING CONFIDENCE

Meeting People
The key to helping your dog overcome these issues is to tackle the fear related to them because this is the essential problem behind the concern. Before examining how to do this, it is important to identify the triggers. This will not only help you to understand where this behaviour is coming from; it will also help you to avoid it happening in the future by knowing where to lower the intensity of interactions while reinforcing a new, increasingly confident response. The following points are guidelines to help you tackle the concern head-on.

- Watch your dog carefully and note down what triggers motivate the concern; urination behaviour and the fearful signals described earlier are cues. Include as much detail as you can, remembering that dogs are masters at detecting and noticing body language; the small details may well make the difference between a successful or unsuccessful interaction.
- Avoid flooding; don't force your dog into a busy room full of strangers if this is his ultimate concern. Build gradually instead.
- When you or your visitors are approaching, try not to rush up to your dog and lean over him excitedly. Instead, allow him to approach you at his own pace and greet him affectionately but calmly. Sitting down first can

be a good way of lowering the intensity of these reactions. If the fear is high then it is advisable to let others know, both indoors and outside the home. Saying 'My dog is very fearful, please keep your distance' can be a good way to let others know not to stroke or lean over him.

- Try to keep vocals soft and neutral and to refrain from shouting or speaking sternly, especially when close to your dog. Keep an eye on visitors, especially young children who may be particularly noisy.
- Try to keep your body language soft and neutral as well, while remaining aware of your dog's signals; then you will be receptive and vigilant if fear or tension grows. If tension begins to grow, reduce the intensity of what you are doing, giving your dog more space.
- Many fearful dogs find being stroked or patted on the top of the head particularly threatening. Take care to keep physical interactions mild and unthreatening and stroke your dog on the shoulder or side of the head rather than the top. Grooming and close handling can be real causes for concern, so once again remember to build the intensity of interaction gradually, rewarding calm behaviour throughout.
- If submissive urination does occur, try to ignore the behaviour rather than rewarding it with sympathy and, as already mentioned, don't punish it as this will only exacerbate the problem.

The next section will show you how to build your dog's confidence around the fear-provoking stimuli. Confidence training exercises are all about helping the

This dog is confident being handled and brushed with his owner leaning over him. Dogs fearful of handling may show concern; therefore, standing side on rather than behind is advisable.

THE KEY POINT

The key to reducing fear during introductions and greetings and eliminating behaviours resulting from it (such as submissive urination) is to avoid eliciting the behaviour in the ways suggested, and simultaneously building the dog's confidence. This covers the PPMRR plan discussed earlier (prevent practice, manage, retrain and reinforce). The most effective way to increase a dog's confidence level is not only to adapt your own behaviour, but also ensure that your family and even visitors are aware of what to do. It is vital that every time your dog meets somebody they take care to remain as passive and unthreatening as possible and allow your dog to approach in his own time.

dog feel calm, confident, relaxed and happy in his skin. This has a huge benefit: the more relaxed and confident your dog becomes, the more likely he is to cope with changing situations and scenarios. Obviously the more intense the fear the harder this is to achieve, but the principle remains the same.

CONFIDENCE BUILDING

Simple Beginnings

The first thing to remember is that confidence building activities and training are most successful if you use buckets of positive reinforcement. This is simply because this kind of reinforcement influences positive emotions and feelings of happiness and well-being – the ingredients of confidence! The key to getting this right is timing: rewarding the dog for showing desirable behaviour and guiding and encouraging him to behave this way. This can be structured in the form of training exercises and commands (a great way to start) and by random rewarding for behaviours you find 'good'! Structured training works best when it is short and fun; finish before boredom or tiredness take over and interrupt the positive energy on both sides. Remember, you don't have to be teaching your dog anything in particular other than being happy and confident. You can begin this by going through your dog's known repertoire of sit, down and give paw. As long as your dog is getting something positive from these interactions and is confident while acting favourably, you are going to be achieving success. Adding simple reward-based exercises can be a great start to building your dog's relationship with you. The next stage is to trap this calm energy and refocus and re-train the dog's fearful response.

ALTERNATIVE REMEDIES

There are various products available on the market that are designed to balance and reduce stress and fear. Bach Flower Remedies™ have been used for many years to help both people and animals cope with their concerns. Herbal remedies have been recognized as effective tools in dealing with many concerns and a qualified Bach Flower practitioner can even mix you a specific remedy for the issues you are having. DAP™ collars and diffusers are fascinating devices which release relaxing pheromones similar to those produced by lactating female dogs. Consult your vet for more information on alternative remedies; many have a ready supply for sale in their centres.

Fear Prevention

Here is a five-point plan for the management and modification of fear.

1. When fear strikes, try to stop what you're doing or guide your dog to a safer position to avoid 'flooding' the senses. If he becomes panic-stricken, calmly guide him further away until he begins to relax.
2. Try not to make a big deal of this; don't reward him or try to calm him with praise as this may lead your dog to believe that this behaviour is desirable. Also don't punish these actions as this will contribute to the fear and stress he is experiencing and can teach him to be afraid and build a negative association. The key is to try and stay calm, neutral and confident and control the situation. You have the upper hand mentally in these cases, so use it!
3. Try not to make your dog face the fear until he has calmed down and is in a

The hand coming towards this frightened collie is too much for her; she has turned away signifying she can't cope with the interaction, especially as she is restrained on lead.

position to learn a desirable response to the situation, remembering again that dogs find it very difficult to learn when stressed. Recall what was discussed in Chapter 2 and help your dog to learn a positive association with the fearful stimulus and become calm and confident when facing it.

4. Lower the intensity of the repeat introduction. It's so much easier for your dog to remain calm and confident while being rewarded for this behaviour if you reduce the pressure and literally allow him greater space and freedom from the point of concern. In this way the dog will be more likely to remain relaxed, accept reward, and learn that there is no need to be concerned. If you are out on a walk you can even guide your dog in circles to help him focus away from the frightening stimulus, and reward him when he focuses on you and remains calm (*see* Chapter 12 to see how to super-train the 'watch me' command).

Here the same collie is playing more confidently (ears up!) and relatively close to a person.

5. Don't forget to reward what you want him to do – give him an option! It is easy when things go wrong to become fixed on the problem behaviour and consistently nag a dog not to do the 'bad' action. The last of my keys to success is not to forget to help and encourage your dog to behave in an alternative way, whatever that may be. For example, your dog is frightened of the television. Rather than solely focusing on the problem, reduce the sound on the TV (lower the intensity), encourage him to come closer to it at his own pace (off lead), and ask him to sit calmly and confidently closer to it, rewarding him along the way. Focus on what he can do rather than what he can't; this will help you to modify his behaviour much more effectively than always thinking about the negative side of things.

TEACHING CHILDREN

When you come to modify your dog's problem behaviour, it's important to remember that the way you, your family and other people act is very influential in this process. Consistency is vital to shape behaviour and even one person's inconsistency can break the chain of success. I have discussed how to help your dog overcome his fear by being careful not to push him too far and keeping human body language neutral. I want to end this chapter with guidelines for parents on how to instruct their children to behave around dogs.

Those of us whose teeth are set on edge by the high-pitched screams of toddlers in supermarkets will have no difficulty in understanding that a fearful dog could be equally upset by the same thing. Dogs are happiest when they know what is going on and the unpredictable movements of young children can be extremely upsetting, particularly when targeted on the dog. An untrained child may pull a dog's ears or tail, jump on his back, persist in chasing him, and has even been known to scream in a sleeping pet's ear. Any one of these actions could make your dog feel threatened.

I believe it is very important to train your children to be safe with dogs. Children are one of the major reasons that dogs are taken to rescue centres, often because the dog has become afraid of the child. When escape is perceived as impossible, the dog is programmed to issue warning growls or snarls, and the situation may escalate and become very grave indeed. I would not hesitate to contact your vet and behaviourist as soon as possible if you see any concerning behaviour towards your child. What follows aims to give you the tools to prevent this situation occurring.

Firstly, it is vitally important never to leave any dog alone with a child. Teach your children how to behave around dogs (and vice versa), but always ensure that you are present to monitor the situation at all times. The next key points have been selected to prevent fearful association developing on either side.

It is important that your child learns not to do the following.

- Poke the dog's eyes and mouth, or inside his ears.
- Pull the dog's tail or legs.
- Run around your dog if he is getting over-excited, mouthing or jumping up.
- Shout around or at the dog.
- Disturb your dog when he is in his bed or quiet area.
- Touch the dog or his food when he is eating.

Children's behaviour can create fear for many dogs, who can't work out and understand their actions. The black and white springer spaniel in this photograph has a worried expression.

- Shout near the dog while he is sleeping, as dogs can become frightened if they are woken up suddenly
- 'Hug' the dog if he is nervous. Some dogs do not like being grabbed around the neck because it can make them fearful and potentially defensive.
- Stroke or pat your new dog without asking or letting them know you are there. Let the dog come to you rather than rush over to them.
- Stay near the dog if he freezes, stares, growls, lifts his lips, backs away or raises the hair on his back. It is very important that all members of the family, but especially children, know that these signals are potentially hazardous.

The key point of these instructions is that both children and dogs need to learn to respect each other through training and positive reinforcement. In this way a fantastic relationship can be produced, with affection and trust on both sides.

9 AGGRESSION

Displays of canine aggression can be absolutely terrifying, whether they are directed towards you or not. The anxiety that accompanies the owner of an aggressive dog can be extreme, often because of the fear produced waiting for the next 'outburst' to occur. Before moving on, it's important to highlight again: if you think your dog is going to bite someone or something or has already done so, you must make an appointment with a vet for your dog to receive a full health check. In this chapter I aim to throw light on this subject while giving you ideas for management and modification that you can use alongside professional advice. It is, however, always recommended that for aggressive com-plaints you seek professional help from a behaviourist, who will conduct a full assessment of your dog's behaviour at first hand to make certain that you are addressing the correct cause of the problem.

TYPES OF AGGRESSION

Throughout my work as a behaviourist I find two major types of aggressive behaviour cropping up repeatedly: aggression towards people and aggression towards other dogs. These two directions can be further sub-divided into:

- Aggression directed at known people or dogs (the owner and family) and

---

A SERIOUS NOTE

Although there are many cases where the aggressive response can be retrained and successfully modified, there are undoubtedly dogs that pose such a threat to society that future behaviour modification and training is no longer safe or advisable. Your vet and behaviourist may determine that euthanasia is the only available and sensible option. I can't continue without stressing that the severely aggressive dog that poses a real threat to people or other dogs must be assessed very carefully. If the aggression presented is high, welfare a concern, or the dog either can't be managed effectively or the modification prognosis by professional assessment is poor, euthanasia may be the most sensible and responsible decision. It's never an easy decision and should never be made lightly, but you must use the vet's and behaviourist's expertise to help you at this traumatic time. The important thing to remember is that the sooner you tackle these concerns the greater the chance of successfully modifying them. This chapter is dedicated to helping you not only to understand the aggressive response in general but also to spot the early signs. I want to help you shape your dog's emotions and behaviour at this critical time – which may make all the difference in the future.

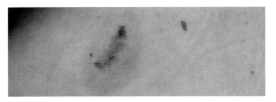

Potential signs of aggression can be terrifying, and actual offensive moves such as snapping, nipping and biting even more so; they can all inflict injuries like this.

covering resource-guarding and conflict/survival aggression
- Aggression directed at strangers (whether people or other dogs, and both in and out of the home) and covering fear and territorial aggression.

There is a final category covering aggression caused by predatory influences. Predatory aggression most commonly occurs outside the house (*see* Chapter 7) but can spill over into inside environments.

SIGNS OF AGGRESSION

There are several signs of aggression, which fall into three categories: potential, defensive and offensive.

Potential Aggression
The potentially aggressive dog may display many similar signals to the frightened dog and this is why it is vital to take note of these signs even if they are slight. Freezing, staring, glaring and showing the whites of the eyes (sclera) are the first indications that all may not be well. Other signs can include:

- Snarling
- Growling
- Barking
- Lunging (without making contact).

These signals relate to the 'warning stage' of an aggressive response but nevertheless should be taken very seriously. If you can identify when your dog feels that he has to warn you, other people or other animals that all is not well, you have gained a valuable tool. It is so much easier to manage and modify aggressive behaviour if you are aware of the 'lesser' signals before the dog intensifies his reaction. When a dog growls he is communicating an emotion, trying to tell you that he is not 'confident' about a situation. Growling, snarling and barking are the dog's way of letting the source know it should 'back off/keep away'. Remember that stress often entwines this system, so it's important to look out for that as well.

Defensive Aggression
The next part of the aggressive response often involves defensive acts but these must not be confused with early signals of predatory aggression, which can be similar but are only present when prey animals are in the vicinity. Defensive aggression behaviours include:

- Snapping
- Nipping
- Lunging in and out quickly.

I have seen many frightened dogs brought to me with defensive aggression concerns, often displaying nipping behaviour (snapping and nipping directed to the backs of legs and similar areas). Many fearfully aggressive dogs nip people from behind because they lack the confidence to move this close head-on. Chasing and herding breeds commonly display such signs due to genetic and behavioural influences.

Signals of defensive aggression are

Potentially aggressive signs can involve the dog's whole body (seen in the black and white collie).

often quick: dogs display flashes of offensive action but recoil rapidly. Nevertheless, these signs are not only frightening, but can do damage and by this stage things have absolutely gone too far. Dogs that are experiencing acute fear and stress commonly display defensive aggression and often remain in fearful positions. They may hold their bodies low, often leaning backwards ready to move away if needed. Defensive aggression can have an obvious cause but can also be the product of a learnt response without many warning or potentially aggressive signs. This is where things start to get much more complicated.

Offensive Aggression

Acts of offensive aggression include:

- Lunging without recoiling
- Biting
- Repeat biting
- Grab, hold and crush bites
- Ragging
- Reluctance to let go.

Offensive aggression is very serious and when behaviour gets to this stage it is often severe. Offensive aggression can be motivated by an extremely fearful event but is more commonly related to learning, because this is the last stage of dog aggression. The previous stages, including the warning and defensive actions, may have been bypassed through repeated learning or because the stimulus is of such a high threatening value. Predatory aggression at this level comes from a different motivation but is equally serious. It often relates to other animals, commonly smaller than the dog in question. The attachment status of a dog who is offensively aggressive for reasons of fear and experience is likely to be insecure and quite possibly confused and disorganized. Owners may find that their dog has contradictory greeting behaviour: one day friendly, the next hostile, and another day fearful. Such dogs tend not to follow any particular pattern and their aggression can appear random, without a particular cause. These dogs need extremely careful professional assessment and veterinary supervision, and a plan to manage and modify the

129

situation carefully while highlighting the potential risks involved, in order to evaluate the best course of action.

CAUSES OF AGGRESSION

Ill-health
As discussed in Chapter 1, aggression can be caused by various health-related concerns. Epilepsy, including idiopathic (no known cause), endocrine disease and various pain-related complaints can cause aggression, sometimes severe in nature. True unprovoked aggression, sudden and out of the blue in nature, can be linked to mental health problems. Such cases often 'forget' episodes as soon as they have occurred and act normally soon after the events. They may have other symptoms such as petit mal seizures (when they stare into space, have glazed eyes and appear to be focusing on nothing). Such dogs need medical attention as soon as possible and this highlights once again the need for veterinary diagnosis and suitable treatment. Attempting to modify such concerns without treating the underlying ailment or at least taking it into consideration is never advisable or useful, and certainly unlikely to help. For example, picture Bob, an adult lurcher who has developed severe handling

Despite the hound mix on the left making a very relaxed and calm approach, the little terrier (right) is tense and clearly lacks confidence.

concerns, showing aggression when his legs are touched. Veterinary examination shows that Bob has a slight green-stick fracture in his leg through over-exuberant off-lead play. Behaviour treatment may well help him through and after this time, but until the leg is treated the odds are stacked firmly against successfully treating the problem.

Fear, Experience and Genetic Disposition
Fear is a very common cause of aggressive behaviour and can even motivate territorial instances. Interestingly, once an association is developed and learnt it can predispose the dog to behave in a similar way in the future, causing what may be seen as unpredictable behaviour.

This is where it is important to consider experience, so it's definitely worth wracking your brain and noting down any significant events from the past. Negative experiences such as frights, fights and injuries are all examples that need documenting so that you can build up a time line of when they occurred. Another point worth mentioning is that aggression is often used as a last attempt to deal with a threatening situation, and dogs, like other social species, are hard-wired with behaviours, signals and signs to appease and defuse tension. This is why it has been vital to go through in detail what the frightened dog looks like and the behaviours that are displayed. However, one indication of fear aggression is the distance your dog puts between himself and his target; while he is barking or moving around, he is also likely to back away when approached.

When the dog is in a threatening situation, real or perceived, he has several options for how to manage it. As examined earlier, the body is in preparation for this event but the brain may have several

UNPROVOKED AGGRESSION: OLD STIMULI DIE HARD

I once saw a young female terrier leap up into the lap of a person she knew and begin biting and ragging her hand as she sat there. Penny the terrier did this even though the girl remained completely still and didn't even lift her hand. At first glance this event seemed both shocking and without cause. It appeared to occur out of the blue. However, when the exact events leading up to this attack and Penny's history were recalled, the stimulus for this event was found. Penny came from a home that had been struggling with her behaviour for several months. She was a very active little dog that lacked confidence and had begun nipping and biting her owner's hands when handled.

Penny had been party to some harsh training techniques where she was pinned to the floor, dragged to her bed and forcefully picked up and moved. This started a cycle of distrust and disobedience. Penny's attachment became disorganized; she was prone to hyperactive displays, and aggressive episodes occurred regularly when her owners handled her, particularly when on the sofa. The cycle of aggression and punishment continued until her owners came to seek help. Interestingly, the stimulus to the aggression I witnessed was the precise threat which had been repeatedly taught: human hands making contact = pain, fear and threat. Just before Penny had jumped on the sofa and become aggressive, she had been happily moving from person to person for affection. When she reached the targeted girl, attempts were made to stroke her and Penny stopped for a very brief period and snorted. It was then she made her move – not while she was on the floor being stroked

Giles, the dog in this photograph, is very happy to be handled, even though human hands are right round his neck area!

but when she had jumped up to the same level as the hands; this was carried out quite slowly without any potential warning signs. Penny had been taught that hands are threatening, so much so that this association had developed disorganized aggression without an obvious reason.

The important thing to remember here is that the reason behind the concern stemmed from a fear association but became altered and distorted through learning. The key to unravelling it, however, involved treating the cause: changing Penny's association and removing the threat while managing daily life very carefully (certainly banning sofa areas!).

seconds to process what to do. The dog may have learnt that submission leads to the threat giving up or moving away, or that running away helps diffuse the fear experienced. If these options are not available or possible, other reactions may be produced. Confinement, restraint, and even past learning where the dog has been taught that alternative behaviours have or haven't worked can effect what happens. The level of this reaction varies from dog to dog and from situation to situation for all the reasons examined so far.

A dog's genetic make-up influences ease and ability to learn specific behaviours (*see* Chapter 7). The predatory chase aggression commonly seen among chasing and herding breeds can be more prominent in such individuals but the impact of learning can't be underestimated. A similar statement can also be made about breeds historically used for fighting purposes, but once again, problem aggression is much more likely to occur if experience and learning has

This lovely pure-bred labrador has the friendly disposition for which the breed is generally renowned. This doesn't, however, protect them against the impact of negative experience and learning.

taught these dogs a negative association. A lack of socialization can also cause fear and feelings of insecurity, making it more likely that interactions will cause negative associations. An insight into the cause is invaluable to every owner and brings me to the next and most important section: what to do to change things. The fact of the matter is that any dog of any breed can show aggression; the next stage looks at what to do about it.

AGGRESSION: COPING, DEALING AND MANAGING

Aggression Towards Known People

When dogs become aggressive towards members of their family, and health concerns have been excluded, something has gone very wrong. When the relationship breaks down at this level many of the problems created are rooted in misunderstanding, and for much of the time the learning and treatment the dog receives can be at odds with the behaviour. With medical factors excluded, I have found that fear and insecurity are primary causes behind many of these displays. Even conflict and status-related concerns can stem from this cause, because dogs are taught to 'up the ante' after progressive clashes with their owners.

Food and Resource Aggression

Resource aggression is a very common problem and has historically been put down to status-related concerns. Interestingly, I have worked with many such dogs and found the cause of their behaviour more to do with insecurity than anything else. This may seem difficult to understand when you as an owner are caught up in frightening aggression when you approach your dog while he is eating or try to take a toy from him. However, the key to understanding this is to ask in each case why your dog feels he needs to guard any of his resources. Hunger, past deprivation, and negative experience, such as harsh treatment and punishment inflicted for not 'giving the item up', are prime causes that I see repeatedly. These teach the dog not only to guard the resource but also to guard themselves – which if you think about it is a double dose of survival behaviour! It's quite easy at first glance to assume that the root of the problem is related to status, but you must look into your dog's perception of each resource's potential – the importance it has for him to guard and protect it. Any one of the factors stated can increase the value of the resource, as well as the negativity associated with your presence near it. In some of the worst scenarios I have seen, dogs have been party to all three causes: deprivation, learning and punishment. I have also seen some dogs adopt alternative resource-guarding behaviour directed, often fiercely, towards places of safety. I noticed that one of the most severe food-guarders I have worked with was shaking, trembling, and had a lowered tail and body posture while bolting his food in anticipation of his owners taking away his food or punishing him severely. He was clearly terrified each time food was presented to him, due to the experience he had been through, but the food value was high enough to keep his nose in the bowl. Such dogs are in real conflict and you must treat them with extreme caution because of their emotional instability. I've visited dogs that have been hit, kicked, dragged, pinned and jerked with choke chains for potential and actual aggression related to resource-guarding, and in every case the behaviour has just got worse. My aim is to help you avoid

this happening, shape the behaviour of everybody concerned, and successfully tackle this concern in everyday life.

Retraining and Modification
It's important to bear in mind the key points of helping the resource-guarder overcome this concern: firstly, reduce the value of the resources; secondly, teach them that there is no need to feel threatened or concerned by close proximity; and thirdly, enable them to actively learn that giving up non-food resources is a positive thing to do. The following techniques show you how to train this association.

Plan of Action: Food
- Ensure that your dog is fed the correct amount of food for his age, breed, sexual status and activity level. Consider increasing the frequency of feeding to twice or three times daily but keep the quantity the same. Increasing feeding times helps your dog to feel fuller for longer and lowers the resource potential of food.
- Change his bowl for a tray or plate – replacing the food bowl with another feeding station can be really useful for beginning to alter the dog's association.
- Change the feeding station and avoid feeding in a corner as this can add to the dog's defensive emotions and actions.
- While it is important to encourage chewing for the feel-good emotions associated with it, try giving your dog food items that are edible in one sitting rather than large objects that he may be inclined to hold on to or guard. The size will depend on the severity of the concern, but definitely avoid large bones and harder chews in favour of softer, smaller treats.

- Give your dog a break and make his food up out of sight, put it down and leave him to eat alone for a set time; do this for at least three days in order to begin with a clean slate. At this stage, call your dog away from the food room and pick up the bowl or tray when he is out of the room and can't see you doing it. Don't take food directly from the dog as this will only add to insecurity. The following training plan shows how to move on from this stage and really help your dog to go to the next level.

Training

The next stage of helping your dog overcome this problem involves actively teaching a different association around the food area itself. Many people try taking food away in mid-mouthful, putting their hands on it and making the dog give it up – with dire consequences. This isn't surprising when you consider that this course of action may well make an insecure dog act defensively and offensively. Once again this has little to do with status and more with their past experience and maintenance state (such as weight and hunger level). My plan works in the opposite way and involves adding food and thus teaching the dog positive association with you in the presence of food.

- Practise the training at least once a day out of the two or three feeds.
- When conducting the training sessions, split the feed station into two and lay down two towels or mats to mark these areas (you should also put down two trays if possible). Keep this area out in the open where you have been feeding your dog.
- Have your dog's food ready in a pot or cup (the type you use to measure your dog's food is useful).
- Next, direct your dog to target the first station using the command 'mat'.

This dog is dipping his chin and turning his head while carrying his toy in close proximity.

In this picture his head is raised and his posture is more confident. Holding another toy or treat to exchange for the toy he has is a great way to encourage and build this confidence.

Walk to the station and help your dog by standing close to it. Ask for a simple sit and then drop some food on the tray for your dog to eat. When you start the process just drop a few pieces (two to four kibble bits), then add more as you progress with the exercise. It may take a week before you start dropping larger amounts; remember that the less you drop the less intensive the exercise is for your dog. You want to increase the frequency gradually, never giving your dog enough to make him feel insecure about your presence. If he does become concerned, you've gone too far too soon. Remember that a cupful of food has much greater value than two pieces and you will have to work up to this.

- Back away when you have dropped the food and move to the next station and repeat the same action: call your dog to this area when he's finished at the first station, ask for a sit position and drop the food again. Carry on until all the food is gone and don't forget to call your dog out of the room before picking up the feeding stations.
- As your dog progresses you will be able to reduce the feed stations back to a single place and put the food down normally as your dog learns that you are not a threat but a positive addition. The goal is to be able to continue normal activities while your dog is eating. I never recommend taking your dog's food directly from them; and it's important to allow them space.

Other Resources Such as Toys

Don't punish dogs if they have items you want and are guarding them or not freely letting them go. You will just make matters worse, teach them a negative association, and intensify the behaviour. Start swapping instantly and don't encourage these actions (they are not desirable, it's just that dogs aren't capable of understanding their emotional implication; modification requires understanding).

If your dog takes toys and hides or guards things, don't leave them around all day long; instead, bring different items out for playtime and swapping games. These can be reduced as the resource potential is reduced, when training begins to teach a different association. Ensure that the toys you have are different, with a wide variety so that your dog has a selection to choose from.

Training

All dogs at some point or another get hold of items they shouldn't have, some of them even potentially dangerous to their health. Swapping is the key to unravelling this, and in order to tackle it successfully it is vital to create short training sessions to teach it. This works in two areas: when dealing with the possession of something, you need to get it off them as soon as possible! And in the meantime teaching them how to do this makes it second nature to them when real events occur.

- At least once a day practise swapping games. Take several toys (all of similar value), a pocket of treats and your clicker ready for the game.
- Practise giving your dog a toy and encouraging him to drop it in exchange for another. Games of fetch are an excellent way to start this. You can also use treats in a similar way: offer a treat in exchange for the toy.
- Don't chase your dog round or follow him underneath furniture as these are

defensive acts. Instead, call him to you and don't carry out the swaps until he does this.

- If he gets hold of something really valuable to him you may have to throw the treat beside him at a slight distance to get the swap.
- Merge these training sessions into 'leave please' commands and as you progress, teach the dog to drop the object and back away a few paces for the reward.

CONFLICT AGGRESSION

Conflicts can occur at any time and often do so when dogs refuse to do what they are told. It's important to remember at this stage that your dog is unable to understand the importance of certain commands and the emotional implications of doing or not doing them. Areas where conflict occurs often relate to going to or on areas that they shouldn't, such as sofas, beds or, in some houses, certain rooms. Much of the time conflict aggression has been caused by previous experience, and punishment is a very common reason for these presenting signs. They often start with the dog's refusal; he may lie down, look away, or even go in a different direction. I'm not denying that these actions aren't both undesirable and aggravating to say the least, but successfully modifying these concerns doesn't need you to become aggressive.

Action Plan

The plan revolves around two areas: effectively handling conflicts when they occur, and teaching new behaviours while building security and changing threatening association with owners. The overall goal is to have an obedient dog

---

WHEN GROWLS BECOME BITES

Rudy was a ten-month-old neutered Staffordshire terrier that his owners had had since he was nine weeks old. His behaviour had progressively got worse from puppyhood and their system of training had taught him some very bad habits. The family had been inconsistent in allowing him on the furniture as a puppy and then banning him from using it as he got older. The ban's inconsistency led to confusion and repeated conflict, resulting in harsh treatment which the owners believed would put him 'in his place'. Unfortunately it just taught him to be aggressive and daily conflict became the norm. When Rudy's behaviour wasn't acceptable, he was commonly sent to other areas, which left him hiding under and on furniture to feel more secure and displaying snapping and biting when people tried to get him out.

Conflict aggression is often worse when any of the dog's maintenance behaviours or health is in jeopardy, because then their internal state isn't as it should be. External influences such as environment and treatment can't be underestimated and the key to unravelling these issues is to treat each one carefully and thoughtfully every time they occur. I never advise confrontation and aggression; in my action plans for owners, rules, management and consistent training are vital.

---

that can follow commands willingly and doesn't become aggressive when told what to do.

- Whenever conflicts occur, stay calm and process why your dog feels that he needs to act in this way. What past experiences and learning can you think of that may have added to this concern? Back off and say 'OK, let's sort this out sensibly.' Higher-pitched vocals of 'Hey, hey, this way' are so much better than low, severe tones of 'Get here now' – so try them!

- Invest in a training line so that you can if necessary guide your dog to another area without having to hold his collar or get too close for comfort. Never drag your dog or punish him using lead contact because this will totally undo any of your good work and just reaffirm that he should be concerned about your presence and control. Trail the line if needed but don't use it unless absolutely necessary; you are working to achieve voluntary behaviour wherever possible.

- When the dog refuses an act and begins to show potentially aggressive signs, back off and reduce the pressure. Instead of marching up and increasing your intensity and aggression, ask for the action in a different way. Use encouragement but be direct, using tools such as a toy or a treat or even walk away calling your dog to come and walking out of sight. Shaking his treat bag or even bouncing a ball can be a good way to increase his interest and 'win' this battle (especially if you are out of sight). Actively fighting with your dog is much more likely to end in further aggression, distrust and even injury, rather than anything else; and you're likely to find yourself back at the same place in the future. The first retraining incidents are going to be the most difficult, especially if the dog has been practising the behaviour for some time. The key is to persevere and watch for signals that the relationship is beginning to strengthen, with trust forming on both sides.

- I want you to consistently get your dog to do as he's told by using positive encouragement reinforcement to begin with (for example, high-value treats). This is vital to teach the new association with your commands and directions. I want your dog to act instantly on cue not only because it has positive consequences but also because it's second nature for him to do so. The more you can teach this association, the further away the past memories of negativity become. As you progress with the training and reduce conflict, a 'good boy' and stroke will suffice. Randomize reward so that it keeps your dog working for it (*see* Chapter 12 for super-training tips).

- Carry out training sessions to ask your dog to target certain areas when he is told to (mat training works well here). Don't just train around the hazard areas but mix things up. The key is to make this learning fun and as non-threatening as possible. Short training sessions (ten to fifteen minutes) and 'teaching time' when you show your dog new things are a great way to bond and build your relationship.

- Keep rules consistent; if you don't want your dog on sofas and beds (which is advisable) don't let him on there at any time. Keep these areas out of bounds with closed doors or stair gates when you're not there to supervise. Rules are vital but you don't need to enforce them with confrontation and aggression that the dog has trouble understanding. Once again, if you want to be heard raise the tone; be assertive, saying 'We're going to do this now, this way Rover,' but don't threaten your dog. This way you can achieve obedience and a quick response on command without having to always raise your voice or get angry. The more you succumb to these negative emotions and rely on aggression to get your way the less responsive your dog will become to your softer, more subtle tones. Do you really want to have to shout at your dog and frighten him when you want him to do something? The answer to this can only be no, as the consequences are detrimental to everyone.

STRANGER-RELATED AGGRESSION

Visitors

This can be not only an embarrassing problem but also a real anxiety for you and people coming into your home environment. Visitors cover anybody coming into your house or garden that does not live there full time. This aggression can be directed towards family, friends, regu-

This dog is waiting inside his garden even though the gate is open. Many dogs can become territorial through fear.

lar visitors such as post people, and less frequent visitors such as delivery people, painters and builders. Visitor aggression therefore falls into two areas: the house and the garden, and both can be as concerning as the other! Territorial aggression is often directed in this way and is often taught either by negative association or by repeated learning that barking, growling and any other aggressive displays result in the person going away. It's a natural behaviour that is worse in guarding breeds and anxious dogs who feel threatened by outsiders.

It's quite easy to see why so many dogs have issues with the postman. He or she arrives without warning, often abruptly waking the dog and pushing foreign objects through the door. This makes no sense to the dog, who barks as soon as this happens. This often directly coincides with the post person leaving and therefore teaches the dog that his behaviour caused the stressor to leave. He feels better and more confident, so this behaviour is actively, albeit unintentionally, reinforced. A very similar pattern may occur in the home and is often the case with routine nippers of moving legs and snappers and biters of approaching hands.

The following action plan is specifically designed for fear-related potential aggression towards visitors. Once again the plan for dealing with aggression at a higher level should be grounded in successful management, which is also reviewed below.

Action Plan
In the house
• Your first consideration should be management to prevent your dog wherever possible from experiencing the emotion that leads to an aggressive

MUZZLE TRAINING

Muzzle training can be beneficial for several reasons: the two most prominent are safety and confidence. Muzzling dogs can protect both people and other dogs from aggression while helping to protect your dog from 'getting into trouble'. Owners of aggressive dogs may also find that modification can be carried out with greater ease when their dogs are muzzled because it gives them greater confidence. Knowing an aggressive dog is muzzled and can't bite anybody can help you to focus on trapping the positive emotions needed to shape your dog's behaviour favourably. All new equipment can contribute to and cause stress and frustration, sometimes making the problem behaviour worse, so suitable training is always important. Acclimatizing your dog to wearing a muzzle must therefore be carried out before its general use, so I have developed some pointers to how to do this successfully.

Before reading these I must emphasize that basket muzzles, sometimes known as cage muzzles, are advisable rather than the cloth variety that binds the mouth closed. I have seen many behaviour cases negatively affected – sometimes severely – by the use of the 'bind mouth closed' variety. It's important to remember that an aggressive dog, irrespective of the cause, is likely to be potentially stressed when in the proximity of the provoking stimuli. Just imagine the added stress of having their mouths held closed, restricting their facial movements and behaviour. Although basket muzzles prevent the dog from biting because they act as a barrier, when correctly fitted they enable the dog to open his mouth, pant, eat and drink. Dogs can even accept treats through the bars of the larger sizes and overall they are a much more sympathetic and effective way of muzzling dogs.

This dog is confident and calm wearing a basket muzzle that allows him room to pant, take and eat treats and even drink although it prevents him from biting.

Here he is socializing with other dogs (a concern for him) and the use of the muzzle gives his handlers greater confidence to allow him greater freedom to socialize and play.

response. Therefore avoid meetings where the visitor is either coming and going briefly, or doesn't like or isn't confident with dogs. Keep the dog in a safe area behind a closed door to keep everyone safe when you don't have time to create a proper greeting. Limiting social introductions to a few regular visitors and friends (adults only) can be a great way to achieve this. If your dog is particularly concerned by a certain sex, choose the alternative until he has built confidence with these people. Move on to others (including the more concerning sex) but ensure that this is done gradually.

- Teach your dog to target a safe zone where he can retreat to when the door knocks or the bell rings. Make this an automatic reaction and create practice sessions to train this action. An open crate can be an effective safe place in the 'safe room'; focal points of mats and a bed can also help to teach your dog to target this room and remain calm while you open the door. While practising this, ask your dog to wait on the mat while you answer the door. Volunteer family members can be really beneficial for the practice runs!

- Ensure that your dog is left behind the closed door or contained room so that he can't run freely to the entrance. This is where problems are likely to occur and it's vital to stop this happening.

You want to stop your dog practising the behaviour but also learn how to behave in future events. When visitors arrive you are likely to be too caught up in greeting them to carefully control, manage and retrain your dog's actions. This isn't likely to support favourable behaviour so prevent these introductions happening.

- When considering whether or not to conduct greetings between your dog and your visitors the answer will depend on the assessment of the level of aggression made by your vet and behaviourist. In some cases it may be advisable to manage your dog at all times behind closed doors when people come inside the house. The next stage aims to show you how to change the threatening association with visitors but this should only be carried out under your behaviourist's supervision and verification.

- Your dog will be safely in his separate area as your visitor arrives. Ask your visitor (the stooge volunteer!) to take a seat in the most open and relaxed

Training your dog to target 'safe' areas such as towels, mats or beds set aside for this purpose can be a great way to build confidence and control.

This dog is settling down and relaxing behind the closed door.

room in your house. Ensure that furniture doesn't block getaway routes and make the environment clear and open as this will lower stress. Give them a magazine or book to read and ensure that they know not to make direct eye contact with your dog, or talk, stroke or move towards him when the time comes to bring him in.

- On a lead or training line (that is, most essentially, having your dog under control) bring him out of his safe room. You may choose to muzzle him to begin with, depending on your behaviourist's recommendation.

- Before you get into the room with your visitor begin asking your dog to do some simple commands such as sit, paw, make eye contact ('watch me') and perhaps also target mat areas depending on where they are.

- Use clicker reinforcement if suitable for each calm, confident command achieved, as long as your dog isn't showing any signs of concern towards the person in the next room. Be sure to use high-value food rewards to trap the positive emotions and teach a different association. Remember that I want you to encourage your dog to feel happy and confident around your visitor, and food can be a great way to start this.

- Decrease the distance (start in the doorway and move a step at a time) still practising the counter-conditioning commands. If your dog starts to show any potentially aggressive signs take a step back and repeat the previous stage.

- Conduct these training sessions for short periods (ten to fifteen minutes) at a time, remembering that their purpose is to retrain your dog's association with the presence of visitors in your home.

- The next stage involves getting closer to the sitting person but still remaining at a safe distance and under lead control at all times. If your dog pulls towards the visitor in a defensive manner this is also a sign that you need to take a step back. It doesn't matter if you go through the first stage in the hallway and entrance for several sessions, as the key is to start to see a change in your dog's behaviour.

- Any movement from the visitor is likely to add to your dog's concern so it's important that they remain still. And remove your dog from the room when they leave as this can be a particularly concerning area.

- As your dog progresses and isn't showing any potentially aggressive signs at all but remaining calm and confident, you can get closer (still practising the

It's important your visitor doesn't lean over your dog or encroach on their personal space. Even Giles, who is a very friendly and social dog, is concerned with this intensity of interaction.

141

same repertoire). Encouraging your dog to target a mat, bed or even towel area can help him feel safe.

- When it comes to greeting and allowing dogs to meet, sniff and get to know visitors, the way you do this depends on your behaviourist's plan, However, there are some important rules to follow.

1. This where lead control and muzzling may be especially important.
2. Don't ask your dog to get to know visitors unless he has shown consistently positive greeting behaviour and no signs of aggression of any sort.

3. When he sniffs, ensure that your visitor doesn't touch him and remains still.
4. The first time you do this reward him yourself and leave the session at this stage (quit while ahead in all cases!).
5. When you are consistently happy that your dog is starting to show positive greeting behaviour, your visitor can treat him. This can be done by either dropping a treat on the floor (without bending down) or giving you the treat to give to him. Don't allow them to hand the treat out directly to the face or mouth of your dog as this may be too much. You may cause an ambivalent reaction whereby your dog wants the treat and takes it but snaps at the hand through a conflict of emotions. I want your dog to get to this stage only when they are truly confident about the situation.

The final stage involves training the same response while giving your dog greater freedom. If he wants to stay away, let him; don't force an interaction. This is where reinforcing mat-targeting at a distance can help him find a safe place to remain calm. Take care to regain control and teach calm behaviour when your visitor moves or gets up to leave the room as this may start your dog's concern again. Additionally, remember that emotions may rise when the visitor comes back into the room so take care not to forget to have things under control.

In the Garden
An important part of stopping your dog practising territorial and aggressive

Fencing off a portion of larger gardens can be an effective way of controlling your dog's access; especially if they have territorial concerns.

behaviour directed towards passers-by and people coming into the garden is management. If your dog suffers from this concern, don't allow people to wander in freely (lock your gate) and don't leave your dog unsupervised in the garden.

If the aggression occurs at specific times (for example, the post person arriving) and putting your dog inside makes matters worse, then counter-conditioning training is advisable. A long line can be a useful tool to keep control over your dog, and give him a job to do at the furthest distance possible from where the post is dropped off at your boundary box. Sit, down, stay, play and even games of fetch can be a great way to change the emotional reaction to the threatening presence. High-value treats and a clicker are really needed to super-train these reactions. Move closer to the point of concern until you are confident that the association is beginning to change.

The key is once again to counter-condition your dog's response while teaching him that these people really aren't a reason to be concerned. To make this easier ask passers-by or post people not to talk or try and interact with your dog as this may make things much worse!

OUTSIDERS

This is another particular area where muzzling may be especially important, because you can never control what other people are doing. Even a dog that has shown a very occasional fear-related issue can be severely and dramatically affected by outsiders that won't stay away! These issues are most commonly caused by fear or a fear-related experience in the past but once practised can become automatic.

The greatest problem for owners of potentially aggressive dogs in the outside world are the other people and dogs in it.

The key to unravelling the concern involves desensitization and counter-conditioning. Although it's difficult in everyday life to keep your dog at a distance from people out and about, it's really important in this plan. It's not always possible, so knowing how to handle accidental close meetings is equally as important and useful to know. The distance you need to be away depends on your dog's level of concern, but desensitization training works best when you start at the greatest distance possible and move closer to the point of concern only when your dog isn't showing concern.

Action Plan

- Avoid very busy areas where the response is likely to be severe (high streets, fetes and busy parks are potential flooding zones). Making your dog 'get on with it' is unfortunately not likely to help because dogs can't learn positive new behaviour while stressed. Keep this in mind so that you concentrate on trapping the calm behaviour in order to retrain your dog's emotional reaction to people. You don't want to flood your dog with the stimulus that provokes aggression because this will either cause shut-down or suppression, or it come back more severely or cause extreme outbursts.

- Find training spots: pick open areas where you can see around you. Large parks, fields and quiet walks are the best places to start because you can circle away from concern whenever needed. Visit these areas for training sessions and monitor your dog's behaviour each time.
- Conduct the desensitization by lead walking calmly around the area keeping an eye out for people. Use the 'watch me' command to counter-condition the response and keep your dog relaxed.
- When you see someone in the distance and your dog notices, keep the control, ask the commands and put your dog to work. Circling, sit training and even a little jog can help give the body and mind something to do and remain unconcerned. As with the inside plan, get closer to the point of potential concern as long as your dog is calm and unconcerned.

- If you are faced with someone at closer than comfort proximity, remain calm but watch your dog's signals. Use the 'watch me' as soon as you can; if he becomes tense try to distance yourself as much as possible. If he starts to bark or reacts, keep him at a safe distance and move past quickly or circle away. The faster he can recover the less his concern will be; it's a useful sign to look out for.
- Use volunteers to help you and act as 'stooges'. These people can walk backwards and forwards at the correct distance while you begin to teach your dog a positive association with their presence.

DOG AGGRESSION

Dog aggression can be occasional, frequent or automatic (every time and during all interactions). The severity of aggressive actions varies within these zones and can range from slight snapping, nipping and biting right through to crush biting, mauling and choking (by throat bite and constriction). True, severe, and

This photograph shows the large grey dog in the centre warning the approaching dog to back off with a clearly potentially aggressive display.

automatic dog aggression is a very serious problem and it is vital that the owner manages the situation very carefully. As said before, professional advice is needed and the following action plan should be supported by your vet and behaviourist. It is based upon earlier less severe signs and I advise muzzle training and control for dogs with high-level dog aggression.

It's a fact that some dogs don't get on; these can be managed by obedience and recall work to ensure that they stay out of each other's way. I will also show you how to build your dog's confidence and social skills. Defensive aggression often stems from a lack of experience or negative events and the key to helping dogs overcome this relies on similar principles to outsider-related aggression. Desensitization, counter-conditioning and socialization can help your dog overcome his aggressive concerns.

Action Plan

- Start training sessions in quieter areas where you can circle away, and remember to keep reinforcing the 'watch me' to carry out the counter-conditioning. I once worked with a client who began driving her Jack Russell to quieter areas rather than walking down narrow streets where dogs were likely to pass at close proximity. This worked a treat and really helped the dog overcome his issues. Changing the environment where negative associations have been built, even if you can only do this part-time, can be very useful. Keep calm and in a very similar way to the earlier plan for people-related concerns, build the intensity of reactions gradually.
- Practise the same walk and if possible ask volunteers to help you. Walking alongside a dog you know can really

Busy events such as dog shows can pose great threats to dogs concerned by others. Expose your dog to such events very gradually to avoiding flooding.

help to form the lesser degree of positive association needed at the start. Train and reinforce the 'watch me' command (*see* Chapter 12) for counter conditioning.
- When your dog is ready to meet others, stay relaxed and keep tension on the lead to a minimum. Look to introduce him to similar-sized dogs of the sex he most prefers. Play is a great way to learn good new associations, so if this is possible and looks likely, let it happen.
- At this stage training classes can be an additional way to teach your dog new skills in the presence of new dogs, but as said earlier, it's important not to get to this stage before your dog is ready. Flooding is never advisable.

PREDATORY CHASE AND PREDATORY AGGRESSION

This can be directed at many things including other dogs, cats, or anything that stimulates a chase response or a further predatory sequence, such as bikes, skateboards, joggers and cars. The

While the black dog sniffs the terrier on the floor, the hound type (left) displays a fantastic play bow to encourage the dogs to play.

Socializing with a variety of dogs can be a great way for them to learn positive associations.

key factor is that movement is often the trigger. Although predatory behaviour occurs in dogs of any sex and age, those that show intense interest in the movement or noise of children or pets should be closely watched. It can be difficult to modify this behaviour as it is part of the dog's genetic disposition, although learning also comes into play. However, aiming to focus the dog and encouraging him to keep adrenaline levels low can be very useful. The 'watch me' technique can work very well in helping owners with such concerns, as well as super-training the behaviours pertaining to the actions to break the sequence.

Action Plan

- Super-train and super-train some more! (*See* Chapter 12.)
- The key is to break the prey sequence in its first stage, so it's really important that your dog listens to these commands because it's a powerful mechanism that's at work.
- Use toys, treats and commands to direct the attention and also divert the energy rather than suppress it. This can help to avoid frustration building, or redirection.
- Use long lines to aid control out on walks so that you can curb the behaviour.

A long line can help you control your dog even at a distance and is useful for controlled socializing sessions right through to recall work.

10 PROBLEMS IN THE HOME

Dogs have lived alongside humans for thousands of years. Many of the problem behaviours that owners struggle with on a daily basis quite simply don't and wouldn't occur in the more natural environment of tribal communities the world over. Moreover, and ironically, many current problem behaviours are also likely to have contributed to the evolutionary success of both our species! The act of dogs barking to alert people that outsiders are approaching springs to mind. The fact of the matter remains the same, however: modern cohabitation with dogs is rife with potential problems. This is a fact that needs addressing and this chapter reviews the common problems that owners struggle with in the home. My aim is to give you practical advice following the PPMRR principles – prevent practice, manage, retrain, reinforce – to tackle not just the problem behaviour but the cause of it as well. The chapter is divided into the average owner's day, highlighting when certain behaviour issues often crop up and what to do about each one.

MORNING: WAKE UP TIME

Inappropriate Toileting

A very common problem presented to many owners when they wake up in the morning is the dog that has toileted in the wrong place. This is probably the last thing you want to deal with upon waking, especially as you may be in a rush to get to work or start your day. Similarly, those of you who experience this problem repeatedly are likely to receive that sinking feeling on realizing that this problem has become habitual. Tempers can very easily become frayed and this is going to make matters much worse.

When this problem was discussed in relation to the rescue dog in Chapter 6, the following reasons were presented for inappropriate toileting: either the dog does not understand where he is supposed to go (bed and toilet zones are not clear in his mind), or the behaviour is due to stress. There are several other potential reasons behind this problem behaviour and sometimes even a dog who knows where he is supposed to go to the toilet and has been fully housetrained can revert back to urinating and defecating in the house (commonly due to stress or health concerns). It can therefore be a really frustrating issue for everybody concerned. So inappropriate toileting can have different causes, and these often depend on the time of day and interaction; this section focuses on morning time.

There are three main reasons why dogs toilet overnight: the first is an inability to hold themselves in (health concerns fall into this category so a vet check is vital); the second is stress and insecurity when left (for example, separation distress);

and the third is excitement upon waking and greeting.

Action Plan

- Once again, identifying the cause of the problem is the first and in many ways most important part of solving it. Therefore if incontinence or health factors are the cause this must be taken into consideration and treated by your vet accordingly. Urinary incontinence can be the symptom of serious underlying conditions, of which urinary tract infection may be the most critical. If left untreated, urinary tract infection can lead to life-threatening complications. Additionally, if the skin is constantly exposed to urine it can cause secondary problems such as skin ulcers. Keep a record of when your dog urinates so that your vet can make a precise diagnosis. The same can be said for defecation concerns such as diarrhoea, which should be taken very seriously.

- Management should be a prime part of treatment, ensuring that your dog is taken to the toilet regularly and routinely – absolutely after every meal. Your dog's diet should also be consistent and balanced, especially in cases where dogs are finding it hard to hold themselves; adding amounts of scraps or high protein feed at odd intervals can disrupt this system. Additionally, if your dog can't hold himself for very long (a more common concern for elderly dogs), ensure that he is taken out to the toilet as late in the evening and as early in the morning as possible. In these cases management is going to be the most important consideration, so ensure that meal times are early enough in the morning and in the evening to ensure that the dog can digest his food and relieve himself

before being left or shut inside for the night. It is also vital that these dogs know where they are supposed to be toileting, so it is very important to add a command word while using praise and reward for the desired behaviour.

Don't be afraid to go back to basics and start retraining the principles of house-training as you would a youngster. Dismiss thoughts of 'he should know better' or 'she's deliberately being bad' as both are unhelpful and destructive. If there is one point I want to reiterate and keep reinforcing it is that all behaviour (including inappropriate toileting) is the result of a multitude of factors; treating the cause is the most effective way of being successful.

- The second cause of inappropriate toileting, the experience of stress when dogs are left alone, is a common associative problem and will be addressed later in this chapter.

- There are some dogs that respond to happiness or extreme excitement by urinating. This becomes more of an issue when owners greet their dogs with a high energy, vibrant interaction! This can rate highly on the excitement monitor, causing an adrenaline rush that speeds the heart rate and changes muscle tone – including the muscle controlling the bladder. Moreover, try not to forget that the dog's bladder is going to be full after an eight- or nine-hour stint inside. This can be quite a diabolical mix! The key point here is to ensure that you take your dog out to the toilet straight away upon waking rather than give him vast amounts of attention and fuss before he has emptied his bladder. This does not mean that you need to ignore your dog in the morning; instead, greet him calmly with calm vocals while ensuring that going out is the number one priority. It is important to remind all family members of this part of the process because it only takes one person to break the chain and be the cause of more problems. When the morning routine begins, as well as other times of greeting that may be of concern, follow these simple rules in addition to the management plan.

- Don't lean over your dog – this can lead to over-excitement and jumping up behaviour.
- Keep vocals calm and quiet and avoid talking loudly while showing affection.
- Keep handling relaxed and gentle rather than handling him roughly or rolling around (this may relate to younger family members in particular!).
- Keep it calm to reduce adrenaline building and too much excitement.

Leaving Time

The morning routine in many households is filled with hustle and bustle; most people's houses are generally hives of activity. For your dog it can be an especially exciting yet stressful part of the day. This is for three reasons: firstly, having been resting or maybe even separated he is excited upon waking up and pleased to see the family members; secondly, as a busy time of the day you may not have a great deal of time to give out attention; and thirdly, at some stage of the morning or day he will be left alone and has learn this association through repeated experience. It is important at this stage to try and imagine what this may feel like for your dog; he is likely to feel a multitude of emotions. If your dog has been through any change internally or externally (such as moving house) this can be doubly so. Inconsistency and change can cause and contribute to stress for the

dog; he doesn't understand or work out the reasons behind these events. What the dog can and will do is behave according to how he is feeling and this is where the trouble can start.

It is always advisable to keep an eye on your dog in the morning and have a routine that caters for his needs. Feeding, drinking, toileting, safety and exercise are important considerations from a maintenance perspective. If you don't have time to exercise your dog this early in the day then do ensure as a minimum that he has had a chance to go to the toilet (particularly after breakfast), as this is going to make the next stage of the morning (leaving) a great deal simpler. Try to always bear in mind the following questions: Is your dog hungry? Does he have water? Does he need to go to the toilet? Is his environment safe and

Leaning over your dog can lead to urination problems so be careful to let them come to you (sitting down while giving affection can be useful to combat this).

secure? Does he have a quiet place to rest? If you can't answer yes to any of these questions, change is needed. It's a simple plan to start, but if you cater for the basics, the next stage is going to be much easier to cope with.

Separation Distress

I have helped many owners whose dogs struggle with being left alone. When separation stress moves to separation distress, displays typically move from brief episodes of barking that subside quickly to long periods of barking and vocal displays, destruction, elimination behaviour, anorexia, redirection and even periods of self-harming. The spectrum is wide and varied, but the root of the issue remains the same: insecurity. So what does insecurity actually mean? A dog who suffers from an insecure attachment can experience acute stress when left alone. Being left is the threatening situation with which these individuals just can't cope. Causes of this concern can vary from some individuals who are predisposed to suffer having been born to reactive parents, through to others who are experiencing change and loss of their environment. In short, anything that threatens security can cause a dog to develop separation distress. Additionally, dogs that have received frequent punishment and inconsistent treatment can be strong candidates for developing this concern through repeated loss of control and experience of fear and insecurity. The key to helping you overcome this problem is to tackle not only the presented behaviour, by modifying and counter-conditioning reactions, but also the root problem of insecurity. Therefore I have split the plan of action into three sections to show how you can most effectively shape your dog's behaviour and emo-tional reaction

to this common and, for many, unavoidable stimulus: being left alone.

Building Security

Security-building exercises involve helping the dog to learn to be calm, confident and relaxed with and without you. Both the calm programme and mat work (*see* Chapter 4) can be very effective in these cases, to introduce and add new calm and safe zones. This will be particularly useful for when you come to leave your dog alone. You only need to carry out a few short (ten to fifteen minutes) mat and calm training sessions throughout the day to start to build this association. The principle behind this training is to give the insecure dog more choice and opportunity to relax and to encourage them to do this with structured training. Starting to build this association before, after and while they are left alone is a great way of increasing security and general relaxation and helping your dog's levels to remain stable.

Preventing your dog from experiencing the stress and distress associated with being left alone is a very important part of tackling the concern. To start with, therefore, it is really beneficial to note down any external stimuli that cause your dog to start showing signs of concern. Once you know these, take care to reduce their intensity. For example, if your dog reacts when you put your coat on, ensure that all your items are ready by the door and if possible out of sight. This way you can settle your dog and then get ready and leave without adding unnecessary stress. Another effective way to tackle this area is to conduct 'desensitizing' training to lessen the status of these cues. It is important to do this very gradually and pick one item at a time, exposing your dog at a low level he can cope with. Putting your coat on for a few minutes but remaining inside, or even watching television are examples of this. Ensure you reward calm behaviour once again and keep your dog as relaxed as possible. You can gradually build up the intensity of the 'stress-causing stimuli' so that these items no longer cause concern.

Action Plan

For this stage of modification I will go through a practical plan of action that I have used with great success with many clients, some of them with very severe presenting signs.

This stair gate separates two rooms but reduces the pressure of leaving training because the dog can still see you.

- Select a safe area of the house where your dog can be left alone without concern. Choose an area that is quiet. This can be a whole portion of the house such as the hallway, kitchen and living room combined, or just one area, depending on your dog's behaviour and which rooms hold the most valuables! Avoid leaving your dog in areas which hold your best furniture if destructive behaviour is on the cards. You may also choose to separate off the safe area with a stair gate rather than a closed door as this is less intensive for your dog because he can still see through it.

  I highly recommend this course of action because it can help the dog to build confidence much more effectively and learn that being left at a distance really isn't a reason to be stressed. Avoid putting a dog suffering from separation distress in a crate as this can lead to severe distress. Confining them and limiting space in this way can cause horrendous side-effects because it effectively and dramatically adds to the dog's lack of control. I have seen dogs needing veterinary attention after panicking when left in a crate. One little terrier I came to visit used her teeth to bend some of the crate bars and then forced her way through, leaving cuts, bruising and hair loss over her head, body and parts of her legs. I recommend using alternative ways to confine the dog to a safe area (such as a stair gate division in a smaller room), which don't involve closing him in a small space.

- Add choice to the safe area such as an open crate in one corner (you can even cover it with an old blanket); a bed and mat or blanket in another; and even an old towel laid elsewhere. These are the locations where you can develop both mat training and calm work to ensure that your dog not only has a positive and relaxing association with these target points but can also learn to wait at a distance from you while remaining calm.

Offering several 'safe' bed areas in your dog's secure room gives him options to choose where to settle. Giving options can lower stress.

- Once you have established your dog's favourite calm location, you can start the 'stay, leave' training and begin to change the once stressful association. First guide your dog to the area, then ask him to sit or lie down depending on how well he has developed this association. You can start with a sit and teach the down as you progress. When your dog appears to be comfortable and relaxed, ask him to stay and take a pace back. Count to three; move back and reward in the same way you would if conducting the mat training. Repeat this until your dog remains calm and relaxed while at a distance from you, increasing the time from three seconds to five, to ten and so on. Then begin to increase the distance until you can stand several paces away without the dog becoming concerned. If stress strikes you may have gone too far too soon. Take a step back and repeat the stage your dog is happy with, remembering that practising a perfect calm stay at a low intensity is better than pushing things too far and your dog becoming stressed again. This will help you to begin changing your dog's emotional reaction and to train him a different association. This should show you how each practical component leads not only to building security from one end but also retraining the response so that you are tackling the problem at both ends.

This crate is suitable for a small dog such as a Jack Russell. It's been covered with a towel and has a soft cover, toys and chews inside, with the door left open.

It can take several weeks if not longer to help your dog overcome concern relating to this stimulus; recovery time often depends on the severity of the concern. If you can begin to change the emotional reaction from stressed to calm when faced with the threat (being left) and build up the time and intensity gently, you may be able to see improvement in your dog's behaviour relatively quickly. The best way to do this is to break the process into stages and keep training short (10-15 minutes) a few times a day. Also take care not to forget that the training is only part of the process; by making daily life and interactions full of opportunities to build your dog's security you will be in the best position to help your dog overcome this very troubling concern.

DAY TIME

Returning Home: Jumping Up

It's a fact that many dogs jump up at their owners. If a dog jumps up at his owner it is very likely that this behaviour is also displayed towards other people, including visitors and general members of the public. This can be a considerable issue because your guests and unsuspecting people outside may not be particularly keen on getting jumped on! Additionally, even smaller dogs can easily knock or push over children, especially toddlers, which of course presents even more of a concern. The motivation for these dogs varies from excitement and insecurity to hostility; however, the most common initial motivation is excitement. The actual act of jumping up through excitement in greeting is generated by a desire to be as close to you as possible, often at face height, as part of the dog's natural meeting behaviour. Jumping up through

hostility is a very different concern and was considered in Chapter 8. Jumping up is an awkward behaviour that often gets worse when attention on the human side is directed elsewhere. This unfortunately can often coincide with the precise times when you are likely to have your hands full and be distracted.

Unfortunately, the more you are distracted, the less attention you are going to give your dog and therefore the more they crave it! Remember again that your dog is pleased to see you and can't fully comprehend that jumping up may mean that the eggs you've just bought are going to get smashed or that your legs are getting scratched in the process. Jumping up through excitement and the dog's overactive greeting behaviour often gets more extreme when they are feeling insecure through attempts to

Jumping up is a common problem in many households, especially at times when hands are full!

153

appease. This is why you can very easily generate negative feedback by using harsh punishment or even by ignoring the dog altogether. The best way to deal with the problem is literally to train another behaviour when greeting occurs, at the very point your dog would normally jump up. This helps to focus the dog's mental and physical energy rather than allow it to spill over into what is after all a very normal behaviour for the emotions they are feeling.

The plan of action shows you the steps to take.

Action Plan

- Practise repeatedly training your dog to sit in front of you when you are at home. Use positive reinforcement to condition your dog to think that sitting in front of you is the most desirable thing to do. Avoid punishment or pushing your dog down as this will often make them worse through increased insecurity and a desire to get close to you. If your dog does jump up, try to move so that he can't hold his paws on you for long and ask him to sit. Give him a reward as soon as he does but keep it relaxed. For example, when he does sit, try not to over-excite him by lavish and excitable praise. Saying good boy and throwing a small treat on the floor is a great way of stopping him bounding up again for a cuddle, which often results if you go down to the dog's level when he is already excited.

- Practise mock greeting sessions; carry out these 'introductions' in the same way that you would normally come into the house. Ensure that you pre-empt jumping up and ask your dog to sit before he raises his paws!

- Use a handful of treats to start the training; don't forget to have some ready when you come in after leaving the dog alone for a while (he will be more excited at this stage).

- Ensure everybody is consistent. Each member of the family must follow the

Cadging for food can be both irritating and embarrassing, especially if your dog behaves this way with a visitor.

Here Libby is actually attempting to steal the sandwich! This is the worst-case scenario and teaches the dog that it's in their best interest to repeat this behaviour given future opportunity.

training. If one person breaks this rule or encourages it, this will put you back. Ensure that you keep the rewards random so that your dog learns not to expect high value food each time. This will avoid another negative feedback situation if you don't have any food to give him!

Cadging Food

This is often a learnt behaviour when the dog has received food at some time, quite possibly accidentally! It's a very natural action and it's easy to sympathize with how great our dinners must smell to dogs passing by! It is, however, definitely not a desirable action, especially as this behaviour often leads on to stealing food items. Once again it's vital to break this cycle and retrain the response in order to deal successfully with the cause of the issue.

Action Plan

- Ensure you are feeding your dog the correct amount of food; consider increasing meal time frequency but keep the amount the same by splitting the overall daily amount. Ensure the dog has plenty of items and opportunities to chew to help them feel fuller for longer. Hungry dogs are naturally going to be more interested in your dinner, so ensure that you cater fully for this maintenance behaviour.
- Never feed your dog with your food while you are eating. You only have to do this once to teach an association and it's important that everyone is consistent (especially children). Also avoid leaving food unattended on work surfaces as this really may be too tempting and only reinforces the behaviour. Remember that when the pay-off for doing undesirable behaviour is food, it can be a powerful motivator!
- Feed your dog at the same time that you are eating your main meals so that his energy can be directed into his own food. This is a good way to break the cycle during the first stage of retraining.
- If your dog jumps up or begins to cadge, ask him 'off' and encourage him to keep all four feet on the floor. Reward as soon as this happens.
- Place a mat or towel in the problem areas so that he has somewhere to target and keep reinforcing that jumping up doesn't get him the food but staying down does produce reward.
- Wean him off food rewards as you progress but use vocals to let him know that going and lying down is the best thing to do.
- The hardest behaviour to modify is the 'food sniffer', particularly when it's at face height with your dog. This happens more commonly when dinners are on laps, but can nevertheless be a real nuisance. Once again, asking your dog to sit can help him to take a step back, and asking him to lie down even more so. This is a valuable command for this concern because it stops the dog reaching the food, lowers the temptation, and teaches him to do something else.

Mouthing

Mouthing is a common concern and can vary from lightly holding and nibbling hands and arms, to holding tightly and firmly or grabbing any part of a person's body. The motivation and intention is different from aggressive biting, although the difference between the two can become a little indistinct and mouthing is, therefore, never desirable. Dogs

Through positive reinforcement and training Libby is now lying under the table while the people above her can eat their sandwiches in peace – success!

use their mouths on one another in play, particularly as puppies, but many adult dogs also display mouthing actions, especially if they have been encouraged or never instructed to display other behaviour. Dogs that are suffering from stress or have issues with handling can also resort to mouthing, often to communicate to the handler to 'let go'. Stress can also make a dog's skin particularly sensitive and uncomfortable when touched, which can be another cause of mouthing. Additionally, some dogs might be unaware that this behaviour is undesirable because their previous owners may not have modified mouthing in the past and may even have encouraged it.

Action Plan

- First you need to determine as effectively as possible why your dog is mouthing. This can be achieved through observing when the behaviour occurs and if there are any patterns or obvious repetition.
- If it only occurs when your dog is playful it may be simply because he is a little rough and unaware that it is a

problem. Mouthing randomly or upon being handled suggests that he may be stressed or have some anxiety about handling. A dog that is stressed commonly reacts to touch or restraint, but this behaviour may also stem from negative experiences in the past.

- It is vital that every member of the family or household is consistent in the training approach. It only takes one person to ignore or encourage the behaviour, and it will remain, if not get worse.
- Do not punish your dog for mouthing; simply train him to do something else. Punishment can make the mouthing a great deal worse and mutate into a more defensive display because your dog may learn to be fearful or worried about you. This is especially true if he is already wary of being handled.
- When mouthing begins, try wherever possible to divert this energy into something else - offering a toy can be very useful. You can also try asking him to do something else, even go through his repertoire of tricks, rewarding along the way. This can be really useful

for redirecting this tense energy. If your dog simply gets a little 'over the top' in play, stop what you're doing and change the game. This will help him to understand that play stops if mouthing occurs and he should do something else (for example, hold a toy instead).

EVENING

Chewing and Destructiveness

Destructive behaviour can be directed towards any number of possessions, from shoes or toys to carpets, sofas and even door frames. Gardens are also not out of bounds to the destructive dog. Dogs can do a great deal of damage in a relatively short space of time and it isn't unheard of for whole kitchens to be ruined within a few hours. Destructive behaviour can be a by-product of separation distress, although boredom and teething in youngsters are other common causes.

Action Plan

The solution to overcoming this behaviour lies partially in management and partially in training.

- First of all, you should limit the possible damage by removing any items that you would not like to be chewed. This sounds simple but it really is crucial; if you leave a shoe unattended in a place your dog can reach you must understand that it may get chewed.
- Secondly, when you go out, ensure that the dog is left in an area where he can do minimal damage. Make sure that the doors to all other rooms are shut so that things of value are not at risk from mouths and teeth!
- Always have plenty of toys and chews available when you are with your dog and when you leave him alone.

- If he spends most of the day on his own, he may be bored. Reconsider your dog's mental and physical exercise regimes. Are they sufficiently challenging so that he is ready for a rest when he has completed them?

Inappropriate Toileting in the Day

Dogs that frequently toilet while their owners are at home often suffer from confusion (they do not know where they are supposed to go) or scent and territory marking (which is more common in males or if other dogs or strangers have been present in the home).

If confusion is the problem it is absolutely vital to clarify where you want your dog to go to the toilet. This can be done by following each of the steps recommended so far, to ensure that you

- keep actively taking your dog out to the toilet (don't just leave the door open as this may not help)

Destructive behaviour can occur anywhere in the home environment and isn't exclusive to inside the house, as this young dog is displaying.

157

- divide the house into sections – don't leave your dog free to go anywhere.

Scent-marking behaviour is more common among dogs that have arrived in a new home or experienced change, or it can be due to the presence of other dogs and animals or the scent of unfamiliar people (especially those who have other animals' scent on them). Although both male and (this may come as a surprise!) female dogs can display this behaviour it is more common among unneutered male dogs. Change can cause many dogs to become uncertain, increasingly insecure and stressed, which can lead them to mark their 'home turf' as a way to feel more secure about things and control the situation. The key to tackling this concern is part management, part intervention and training. If your dog has scent-marked in the home the first thing to do is try and make home as relaxing and secure as possible – ensuring that you are catering for each of his maintenance behaviours – eating, drinking, sleeping, defecation and urination. If any of these are off-key,

This little chap is scent-marking the tree; this action can be seen in the house for the same reasons, especially in new areas where other dogs have been.

inappropriate toileting and scent-marking are much more likely to occur. Keep a very close eye on the scent-marking dog whenever you can, and when you go out ensure that he is left in a smaller area of the house but a place that is as relaxing and calm as possible, with plenty of choices to go to (several bed areas such as a mat, blanket and soft bed, perhaps even an open crate covered over). While watching you dog, take note of repeated sniffing or circling of a particular area. Watch for 'finding the right spot' behaviour: intent sniffing, often circling to repeat, and positioning themselves carefully, all ready to lift a leg over the chosen spot!

This is a warning that marking may well follow. At this point try to distract the dog with a louder, higher-pitched noise such as 'Hey, hey, this way' and encourage your dog to follow you out to an appropriate toileting location. The aim is to distract the dog not to punish him, as this can lead to further problems! If you can't get there in time the best thing to do is ignore this behaviour and ensure that you clean the area as effectively as possible. This may sound rather odd but remember that the cause of this may well be a lack of security through change or the introduction of a new scent, so telling them off really will not help and is likely to contribute greatly to the problem.

Attention Seeking

Attention seeking behaviour can range from constant touching, sniffing and licking to barking, circling and even nipping when ignored. The cause relates back to security and these dogs often suffer from security issues, are likely candidates for separation concerns, and are generally clingy and lack independence. The key to improving this is again based upon the similar principle of the dog suffering from separation distress, and the plan of action has two main parts: managing your routine, and ignoring the negative behaviour but encouraging favourable actions in its place.

Action Plan

Note when these events occur: the time of day and their content. If barking occurs at certain times then it may be useful to change your routine. I once visited a client whose dog barked incessantly after her evening walk when her owners sat down to watch television. This is the plan they followed to change her behaviour.

- The dog's owners changed her routine so that Flopsey received her evening meal later than before, while they were watching TV. This began teaching a different association and gave her something else to do while benefitting from the dopamine produced by the food.
- They also worked on clicker training to reinforce quiet and calm behaviour, ceasing the clicker reinforcement as Flopsey began totally to relax. Mat training and the calm command were used in conjunction to settle Flopsey, but her owners ensured that they ignored the barking at all times.
- Walk time was moved to just before bed because the walk was contributing to Flopsey's excitement. Also, instead of off-lead play and fetch games, I advised a calm lead walk with some added focus training just to take the edge off her activity level.

Jealous Dogs Versus Mediating Mutts

The jealous dog can be a nightmare to live with and a real concern. Jealous dogs can show episodes of jumping up to separate, nip, snap or even bite other people or animals that come close to their attachment figure (their owner). The onset of this behaviour can be rapid, with different motivators; but the cause is insecurity.

Mediators are dogs that often try to split up and divide people or other dogs. Such individuals jump up and in between owners, or sometimes direct their attention by hostility towards individuals that threaten their security (often by taking attention from them). Examples include owners talking to another dog or stroking it and giving it attention. When a dog perceives someone or something as a threat to them (taking attention or direct concern), the product is behaviour to stop this happening. The key to unravelling this includes watching, acting and training while ensuring that the environment helps reduce the pressure that these individuals experience.

Action Plan

- Keep your environment uncluttered and as clear as possible so that the dogs are not pushed into a small space, which can make them feel more defensive.
- Ensure that each dog's needs are fully catered for; competition for resources will lead to insecurity and further concerns.
- Ensure that each dog receives the same level of attention.
- During times of attention seeking and potential concern, ensure that you don't get in-between the dogs and avoid giving affection if you can see tension building.
- If a dog or dogs starts to freeze stare or glare, interrupt the behaviour or even move away to defuse tension.

11 PROBLEMS OUTSIDE

When your dog's behaviour becomes problematic out of the house it can create a whole new level of concern for owner and dog alike. This is due to two principle factors: it is very difficult to control the outside environment and the other people and animals within it. Problems that occur out of the home environment are not necessarily confined to parks, fields and streets, and this chapter investigates where these potential risk areas are likely to occur, reviews the resultant common problem behaviours that frequently occur out of the dog's primary home environment, and, most importantly, suggests how to tackle them.

Pulling is a problem for many owners and when you have two dogs the issue can be doubly problematic.

PULLING ON THE LEAD

Pulling on the lead is one of the most common behavioural problems when out walking. So why do dogs pull? The reason is very simple: they are trying to get to where they want to go as fast as possible. We have all seen dogs that take their owners for a walk. Pulling on the lead can be an embarrassing and aggravating concern for many dog owners, and it arises from one fundamental principle: putting a lead on a dog effectively teaches him to pull. This may sound rather odd, but the fact of the matter is that dogs learn to lean against the lead in order to get to their destination as quickly as they can. Let us also remember that a lead is a very unnatural device for a dog and prevents him from walking the way he might if he was free to choose. Anybody who has watched dogs off-lead in a park is likely to have seen them running backwards and forwards, walking or trotting along in all directions. Many young and healthy adult dogs would not choose to plod along at the exact pace of their owner because that is not their natural gait. We must therefore be sympathetic to our 'natural' dog and encourage him through training to adopt 'our' technique – remembering, however, that it may not be as easy for him as we imagine!

Training starts with how you, on the other end, respond to your dog's pulling:

to counter this behaviour you should not jerk or wrench the lead when he pulls as this just encourages him to pull harder or hurts them in the process. Instead, you should use the lead to gently guide him. Try the following to see how it works: if you ask somebody to pull your arm, you will find it very difficult not to resist and pull against them. Then get them to guide your arm firmly but gently; this makes it much easier to move in the direction intended by the person guiding your arm. Now relate this to your dog's neck: which is going to be more effective, painful pulling or gentle steering? Pulling generates tension and frustration in both you and your dog; it may also make you angry, which in turn could make you want to punish your dog. Teaching your dog to walk loosely while on the lead takes patience, practice and consistency. Many people give up too soon because they take their dog to a busy park and wonder why he does not listen and is not walking close to their legs. As with all training, it is essential to build the behaviour gradually, which is easier to do when there are fewer distractions. When you feel the command is adequately reinforced, move on to more challenging locations, but do this in small steps. As discussed earlier, small steps are so much easier to accomplish and more enjoyable, because each step gives you and your dog a sense of achievement.

Here Giles is happily walking to heel without a lead in sight. Note his confident and happy expression.

Giles's head is close to my leg in this photograph and he is staying very close with his nose reaching up to the hand.

Action Plan

The best way to train your dog not to pull involves no pain or punishment, but relies on teaching your dog a different relationship with the lead.

- Begin the training in a place with no distractions, not even a destination! Start in the garden without a lead, which makes it more fun for your dog and more relaxed, as no coercion is involved; he is choosing to be with you.
- Encourage your dog to walk close by your side by holding a treat. In a cheerful tone say 'Heel', and if he responds, reward him (click and treat training works well here).
- Take a walk around the garden practising the command while there are few or no distractions. Walk in circles, and if your dog begins to wander, guide him in this circular direction. Give lots of positive reinforcement when he is by your side and ensure that you give him regular breaks to enable him to concentrate effectively.

The next phase is to reintroduce the lead while still in the garden. Hold it loosely and practise the 'heel' command, continuing to click and treat the desirable behaviour.

- When your dog understands the command and it's becoming automatic, take him on the lead out of the garden to a quiet location. This could be a park at a quiet time of day. The quieter the area, the easier it will be to maintain your dog's focus on developing loose lead walking. If he begins to put tension on the lead, use large circles to guide him in the right direction.
- When he no longer pulls on the lead you will be able to go anywhere with him, as you will be taking him for a walk and not vice versa!

Although on a lead, Giles remains walking to heel with no tension. Don't forget to carry on the training even when the lead is attached.

As Giles turns he is directly following me, making eye contact even though the lead is completely loose.

REFUSING TO GO FOR WALKS

A concern that occurs most often with nervous or under-socialized dogs is that once outside their own territory they refuse to go any further. Such dogs are so anxious about the world outside their home that they simply freeze. Putting them on a lead and trying to pull them into action just adds to their concern. Other dogs are quite happy to run about when they are off the lead, but will refuse to move as soon as the lead goes on. This is very significant, as it shows that they do not feel safe on the lead, which takes away their ability to fight or run away.

ACTION PLAN

- As with the problem of the dog pulling on the lead, start in the garden. Encourage him with treats to walk by your side in circles around the garden. Reward even small steps, and keep the session short. You can use toys, treats and affection to do this. This will teach the dog that walking with you is very rewarding and a positive experience.
- The next step is to use the lead while walking round the garden. Don't forget to use plenty of praise.
- When you eventually risk the area outside your garden, put him on the lead (in case he surprises you and runs away), stand in front of him and call to him. If he refuses to move, wait as long as you can and if he makes only a slight movement towards you – click and treat. Make sure you do it while he is moving, not after he has stopped or before he has started. If you cannot manage this, try luring him with a tasty treat, wave it under his nose and as soon as he moves, click and give him the treat.

EXTRA EQUIPMENT

I consistently find that harnesses can really help to alleviate pulling concerns. I commonly use the standard variety that doesn't have any anti-pull functions in order to keep tension to a minimum. I also recommend the use of double clip leads so that you can gain further control over the head and body. These can be organized in several different ways: clipped onto the collar and harness; as head collar and harness; or as head collar and collar. This system can be very useful in changing the relationship the dog has with the lead, and the 'rein affect' can make training easier. Head collars can also help these concerns but like any new equipment can cause considerable frustration. A double lead contact can help to take the pressure off the nose so that you only use the head collar to guide the dog. It's important not to pull hard on the nose area and the harness or collar contact can help alleviate this pressure, giving you other options to control your dog when needed. All new equipment should be introduced slowly with reward training.

Harness use enables you to control two areas of the dog's body through different contact points. This gives the rein effect shown in the photograph.

This dog is chewing on his lead, which may not only damage the lead, but become worse (ragging) in the future

- Gradually increase the number of steps between clicks.
- Once he is able to walk some distance with you, make sure you keep him at a safe distance from anything that worries him, and circle away if you need to.

BITING OR RAGGING THE LEAD

This can be extremely aggravating behaviour! A dog that holds the lead with his teeth and hangs on to it, often ragging and pulling against the owner, is a potential hazard for both the dog and owner. A dog can very easily injure its mouth when engaging in such activity, especially if its teeth catch any metal buckles or fastenings.

This is one reason to avoid chain leads. In addition, 'lead raggers' commonly get very close to their owner's hands when holding on, in their attempt to get greater control over the lead. The motivation behind such behaviour can stem from stress or frustration, or it may even have been taught or encouraged in the past.

Action Plan
- Never encourage your dog to play tug or rag, or even pick his lead up with his mouth. The lead is not a toy or an item to play with. Do not fight with your dog when he rags the lead, nor pull against him; this is likely to make him think it is a game, and make the activity even more enjoyable for him. Avoid playing tug-of-war games with such dogs for the same reason. Have a toy at the ready and encourage him to hold on to this instead.
- If your dog is not interested in the toy, make fitting the lead an exercise in itself; use your clicker and treats to break the process into stages. If he is frantically jumping around, ask him to sit, wait, clip the lead on, and off you go, clicking and treating as he succeeds with each command. Once again punishment is likely to make the complaint worse, especially if the root of the cause is stress or frustration.
- If your dog has become a habitual 'lead ragger' while out on walks, use a toy to divert him. Ensure that the toy you use for walks is separate from all his others, and that it is something he loves to carry. By redirecting the 'ragging energy' you can successfully modify such behaviour. In addition, giving simple commands can encourage the dog to focus and become calm through the release of dopamine in the brain, actively retraining the behaviour.
- If your dog is a very determined 'lead ragger', using two leads can be another useful method. Clipping on two leads, or using the double-clip lead in the manner described earlier, and dropping whichever lead he begins to grab, avoids your unwilling participation in such activities. You will have to be quick for this to work, however.

- If you are out in a field and your dog is ragging the lead and you have no tools to help you, stop moving and wait until he stops before going anywhere else. Always reward him when he drops the lead, however exasperating it is!

OTHER CONCERNS WITH DOGS ON THE LEAD

A large proportion of the concerns people have with their rescue dog's behaviour involves walking on the lead. Owners describe their dogs lunging, whining, screaming and barking, while one lady said her terrier did a 'Flymo' manoeuvre at the sight of another dog! Most of this unwanted behaviour occurs at the sight of an external stimulus such as other dogs, traffic, cats, people or livestock. The dogs become so stressed that they are unable to concentrate or focus. Some owners even feel that their dog is having an attack of some sorts as the dog seems oblivious to everything but the stimuli. Effectively, this is not far from the truth because their dog is experiencing the effects of a surge of adrenaline triggered by the 'fight or flight' response.

Action Plan

- Before you can take action you must first identify the stimulus, namely what causes the behaviour to occur. Having identified the stimulus, you then need to desensitize the dog to it. Do this by exposing him to the stimulus from a safe distance; this will be somewhat further away from the point at which your dog normally begins to react to the stimulus.
- Use the 'watch me' command to keep him calm and focused, and reward him with 'click and treat' when he complies. If he begins to react to the stimulus, you are too close and he cannot yet cope with this level of proximity.
- Take him further away by leading him in a curve, a gentler movement than simply turning back. Then regain his attention with the 'watch me' command.

REFUSING TO COME BACK WHEN CALLED

Trust is an essential component of the relationship you have with your dog, and one of the foundation stones to this is his

This dog is approaching on a recall with great precision and speed.

The happy expression on this dog's face communicates that returning when called is a really positive thing.

returning to you when called. Nothing is more distressing than the thought that you have lost your dog as you frantically call for him. Some dogs may not return when called because they are just too busy nosing around in the undergrowth even to have heard you; others do not return because they know there is no need to come first time because you will keep on shouting until they are ready. Some dogs think that the voice you use means that you are angry with them, and if you are standing with your hands on your hips they are probably right! The most important factor in training recall is that you ask your dog to come to you in a cheerful and friendly manner. Shouting or punishing your dog because it has taken him twenty minutes to return to you will not make him want to come back the next time. It may be frustrating and cause you anxiety and concern, but grit your teeth and put him on the lead, praising him as you do so: in this way he learns that something good happens when he returns.

Action Plan

- Build the recall command in a location where there are few distractions, such as the garden. A volunteer is very useful during this stage, so recruit a helper if possible to be at hand.
- Ask the helper to stand next to your dog, taking the lead from you. Then ask your dog to 'wait' and walk a few metres away in front of him so that he can see you.
- Then stand up straight, open your arms and smile and say 'Come' in a very lively, fun manner. If this word has failed to recall him in the past, then it is a good idea to choose a new word for this new training so that he has no inbuilt associations.

- As he runs to you, keep smiling and when he is close say 'sit', then 'click and treat'. Put your fingers through his collar to make sure he cannot run away. Never grab him as this could cause him to become fearful or defensive.
- Practise recall in the garden, and when you feel he is really getting to understand the command, move on to an outside area. Choose a place free from distractions, or take him there at a quieter time of the day. If the area is not fully enclosed and safe to allow your dog off the lead, a long line can be used. The same principle applies, but as you ask your dog to wait, the helper will hold the line and let out enough line to reach you when you call your dog.

TRAVELLING

Car Journeys

I have come across many dogs that are simply terrified of travelling in cars. Some cases have been so severe that their stress commenced on the slightest cue that a car journey might be on the cards. Travelling can cause many dogs concern for several reasons. Firstly, many dogs suffer from car sickness; this may have begun when they were very young and can be the cause of a negative association that lasts into adulthood. Additionally, I have also worked with dogs that have suddenly developed an aversion to car travel through past negative experiences both in the car and upon arriving at a destination. One dog in question developed a fear of travelling in one of his owner's cars but remained confident in the other. The reason, it transpired, was simple: this car had transported him to spend a night in a boarding kennels. This negative experience became associated with this particular car and stuck firmly in his mind. The following are the presenting signs and displays often associated with this concern.

- Reluctance or refusal to get close to or into the car.
- Stress such as shaking, trembling, drooling (very common with dogs that are or have been car sick or build this association), whining, barking, reluctance to settle, pacing, anorexia, elimination behaviour, heavy panting.
- Some cases may bark through excitement but nevertheless the problem is still very concerning, especially if you have a long journey ahead of you!

The action plan focuses on tackling the dog's imbalanced internal levels. Stressed, very excitable dogs will benefit from relaxation and calm work in the home (*see* Chapter 4) as well as specific car training.

Action Plan
- Essentially, try to look at car travel as three distinct sections, each of them potentially threatening to your dog. The key to unravelling is helping them to learn a different response when faced with the stimulus; this is much easier to achieve by breaking it into sections. Break car travel into:
  1. Getting to the car
  2. Getting into the car
  3. Car travel.
- Tackle each separately, remembering that they are each in fact linked and that if you can maintain and support calm and relaxed behaviour and emotional reaction to the first stage this will have a very positive effect over the second and third. This way you are helping to shape your dog's feelings

and behaviour and form a positive association chain. Breaking this into sections can be very useful as it gives your dog regular breaks from the 'whole event' and avoids flooding and overwhelming his senses. Try to conduct the training when you have plenty of time and don't actually need to go somewhere to start. Obviously these tools will also be useful when you next need to take your dog somewhere in the car, but you are likely to be much calmer and in a better mood for training if you aren't under pressure.

- Stage 1: practise getting ready to go to your car, with car keys and the dog on his lead. As soon as you begin this process monitor your dog's behaviour and gently guide him out of the house. If he becomes fearful, refuses to walk or becomes stressed at any stage, be very careful not to tell him off. Instead, allow him space to remain calm and ask him to do something: simple, easy commands or actions. Circling, sitting and even giving paw for reward can be good ice breakers, remembering that the whole point of the exercise is to help your dog to feel calm and relaxed rather than fearful, stressed or tense. You can also use clicker reinforcement to help shape behaviour and practise moving backwards and forwards to the car. At this stage don't get in until your dog is calm and relaxed. This part of the plan is about tackling the concern related to getting to the car. You can even take a break after this stage, especially on the first few occasions.
- Stage 2: once you and your dog are confident in stage 1, open the car door and repeat walking up to the door without asking your dog to get in. Reward him whenever he is close to the car; try asking him to sit in front, once

167

This dog is happy and confident sitting in the back of this car. It can take time for dogs nervous of car travel to build a positive association.

Breaking car training into sections, counter-conditioning and rewarding calm behaviour are effective ways of helping dogs overcome their concern.

again trapping the calm emotions. Once you have established this, invite your dog to get into the car. You can drop a treat in the car for your dog to see, once again trying not to pull him in as this is likely to encourage him to stop moving. Practise getting your dog in and out of the car without actually closing him inside. This helps not only to continue to change the pattern of learning he may have picked up, but also lowers the intensity of the training.

- Stage 3: when you are really confident that the earlier stages are going well, close the door and wait a minute before allowing your dog to get out again. Practise this, gradually increasing the time. You can keep rewarding your dog here if he is calm and able to take treats and at this stage watch his signals very carefully, once again avoiding flooding. You want him to practise calm and relaxed emotions rather than stress and excitement, so keep this in mind. It is advisable to take a break before the next stage and remember that although this description of what to do may sound lengthy, when actually practising these steps it may only be five to ten minutes! At this point it is time to start the engine and take a turn in and out of the driveway. Increase the time and distance you do this, depending on your dog's capability. If you can seek help from a volunteer to keep encouraging your dog to remain calm for reward, so much the better.

VISITING OTHER PLACES

The Vet

Vet visits can be very traumatic for your dog, for very clear and yet often forgotten reasons: veterinary centres are full of unfamiliar people and animals, some of whom may be stressed or even aggressive, and at some stage your dog is likely to have experienced a painful event. Remember that although slight, injections can hurt; not to mention any other treatments or procedures that your dog may have been through.

Action Plan

- Break the process into sections and if you can, practise going to the vets, getting out of the car but then going home again.
- Make each visit a positive experience and use clicker and treat reinforcement to help build this.
- Ensure that you allow your dog to go to the toilet before arriving at the vet's (a quick walk round a nearby park or garden beforehand is a good idea). This is important so that your dog is comfortable going in, as many dogs may experience a dire need to urinate or defecate when stress strikes.
- While in the vet's stay calm and allow your dog to settle, but don't be afraid to ask for simple commands, rewarding along the way. Remember also to praise your dog for calm behaviour.
- You can even take your dog's mat or a towel for him to sit on, which can be a great way to reduce his nerves. Veterinary centre floors are often cold and slippery, so offering a warmer, soft area to target can be helpful for many reasons.

Everywhere Else

Taking your dog on trips to the pub, fêtes, shows, picnics and even holidays can be the best times away, but it's always important to keep an eye on what's going on. As a last note to conclude this chapter I want to stress that it's vital to judge your dog's coping capacity

Dog shows and other busy events are frightening for many dogs especially if they are worried by people or other dogs.

when you are out and about. Watch out for signs of fear, stress and concern and when these occur be sure to act. If your dog has a nervous disposition don't push him too far by making him go to very busy events or meet people close up when afraid. Instead, don't be scared to ask people not to stroke him, and develop his confidence gradually using the advice and training tips described all through this book. Set up your dog for success, but remember that you have the power to shape the surrounding environment, encounters and behaviour, so use this ability wherever you can.

12 TRAINING FOR OBEDIENCE

WHY CONTROL IS GOOD

Many people can identify with that sinking feeling that occurs when passing by a perfectly behaved dog trotting along at his owner's side. As he displays a perfect heel with not even a whisper of a lead in sight, your dog in contrast is simultaneously dragging you 'which way and that' and choking himself in the process. There is no doubt that obedient dogs are not only easier to live with on a day to day basis but that issues that come along are often much easier to manage and modify. This covers every part of living together in and out of the home.

SUPER-TRAINING

This chapter will help you to super-train your dog in a number of different ways, to the benefit of numerous different situations, and to manage and modify a plethora of problems.

What is Super-training?

Super-training is effectively a method of training where you repeatedly reinforce the required behaviour so that your dog learns to react automatically to the required command. The benefit of super-training is that it produces ultimate obedience and control when needed.

Control is critically important especially in built up areas where roads are present. This dog is automatically waiting before going any further.

MOTIVATION FOR TRAINING

The motivation for your super-training is dependent on your life-style and a combination of needs and wants. You might have a long-haired dog that regularly needs to be clipped and if your dog doesn't like the clippers or will not let you shear him, then that causes a problem for you and your pet. On the flip side you might have a dog who loves to swim in any available water and, as many a dog owner has discovered, the more stagnant the water appears, the more attractive it becomes! In this instance, you really want to be able to bath your dog or give him a quick hose down in the shower, but if he hasn't been used to this in the past or doesn't like it, this too can cause difficulties. This is particularly the case with larger dogs that need to get into the bath under their own steam. This is more of a want than a need but you can quickly see how requirements match, complement and cross over in many scenarios.

As discussed in the previous chapter, vet visits pose concern for many owners. Trips to the vet's, be it for an annual check-up, vaccinations or something more spontaneous, are a prerequisite of dog ownership, and super-training calm, malleable and positive behaviour can be critical. It constantly amazes me that so many dogs spot the vet's uniform and turn into a cringing, scared puppy or potentially a snarling banshee of a beast. Vets of course are used to these Jekyll and Hyde moments, but anything we can do to calm the dog, reassure the dog and control the dog is a very good thing. I examined how to take effective control of the situation, bringing super-training into the mix to show you how it can relate to specific events. The key being that you super-train the desirable behaviours and emotions repeatedly to help your dog cope in practice and reality with the various situations he is faced with.

From visits to handling concerns, this conditioning can be useful, changing a dog reluctant to have his feet touched into one who enjoys the process, making brushing into a pleasurable experience, and recall a fun, rewarding activity in its own right.

ABOVE: With clicker and treats at the ready you can super-train behaviours you may have thought impossible in the past.

LEFT: Even super-training superficial behaviours such as paw commands can be incredibly useful when you need to handle your dog.

This can be very beneficial for dogs that have learnt behaviour over months or years, particularly when learning has become habitual. These dogs often act before thinking, a characteristic that covers a wide range of behaviour problems. Super-training blocks that instant reaction and converts the dog's behaviour into another action, thus helping to prevent a recurrence. Super-training conditions behaviour responses and can make the difference between successful rehabilitation and failure. All through this book I have shown the numerous factors that lead to and cause problem behaviour. Super-training works most effectively alongside the action plans described, providing the final 'icing on the cake' to behavioural modification.

What to Train?

The normal variants of super-training come in two groups but both are fundamental in helping your dog reach his full potential. I use this method throughout my work and it can be modified, tweaked and tuned to cater for each dog's individual needs and personal characteristics. First on the super-training list of behaviours are the basic commands: sit, down, and stay. Super-training even one of these actions means that you have a command you can rely on in most situations, even if they are out of the ordinary. The second group is normally specific to your problem dog's behaviour and includes commands such as watch me, calm, target work and come. Of course the sky really is the limit in what you can teach your dog; however, these behaviours are specifically selected for their use in counter-conditioning and general obedience. The first super-trained command is the critical one because it sets the pace and direction for all training afterwards, and can dictate future success or failure. Pick something that is easy for both dog and handler to work on, with the need for repetition carefully balanced so as not to become monotonous.

The tools of your trade will be two types of treat: one high value (for example, a small piece of chicken or hot dog cut up small) and one of normal value (for instance, a piece of the dog's normal dry food). The third and critical piece of equipment is the clicker. As discussed earlier, the clicker is an invaluable tool for any dog trainer because it allows you to reward the desired behaviour in a specific and powerful way when paired correctly. Additionally, don't hesitate to use your dog's favourite toy as a reward; tennis balls and even footballs make great rewards.

TEACHING

Randomize the value of the rewards and, to mix things up, every now and again give an extra amount of food when the dog behaves favourably. Avoid this extra giving at the end of training as your dog may become used to it and stop working on receiving it at another time.

To really work your dog's brain and start super-training the first basic actions, limit your commands to single words and let him work out what to do next. Add pauses and wait for him to work out the desired behaviour. Don't give the reward until the select behaviour is performed, but remember that you must repeat an easier command in between if frustration strikes or he gets confused. Otherwise you may topple into the realm of negative reinforcement, which can slow the learning and the enjoyment of training. The key is to shape actions by giving triggers and pointers at the start and then single commands, so that an automatic reaction can be conditioned. Body lan-

Here Giles is having his ears examined, which is a vital part of health care.

Toys such as your dog's favourite ball or ragger (pictured) can be fantastic rewards and motivators while super-training.

Conditioning and super-training the sit command can have so many uses.

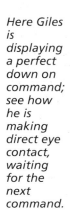

Here Giles is displaying a perfect down on command; see how he is making direct eye contact, waiting for the next command.

guage can serve as an excellent way to trigger your dog's behaviour; I find repeatedly taking a step forward and raising the hands while asking for 'sit' is invaluable when the dog gets confused. Introduce hand signals, facial expressions and whispers so that even the slightest cue will cause your dog to perform the behaviour straight away.

The basic process for any super-training is the melodic way that every command is followed by a reward in order to condition the response. What you should aim to achieve is a pre-programmed response so that desired behaviour becomes automatic on command. The key to this is much easier to do poorly than correctly, and more than half the battle is that you and anyone else training your dog need to follow the principles to the letter every time you start super-training. As the old saying goes, always be prepared, and make sure you have a little pack of the things you will need. You can buy a small pouch from most good pet shops that is specifically designed to hold treats for your dog and can normally be attached to your belt when out and about. This same set-up can be used to attach a clicker, and now you are ready to begin super-training your dog.

Sessions should not last any more than ten to fifteen minutes; as with many people, dogs can only take so much in at one session. Ideally this is fun, but it most certainly needs to be a 100 per cent positive experience. If at first the dog does not pick up the command, you must not get annoyed or angry. This is going to take time, which could mean months to get it accurate and continuous without failure. As I have said before, the need is for correct practice and repetition, not monotony. If boredom begins to strike, take a short break to avoid frustration

building on each side. Find out what motivates your dog most effectively and keep it random, as this is going to be a key factor in the conditioning and its long-term effect. Your dog might prefer chicken to sausage, dry to wet, or something very specific to him or her. If you can find out what that is, then it becomes much easier to achieve positive results in a shorter period of time. This is teamwork and the more you invest, the more your dog will want to improve and the harder the dog will work to get that improvement. After ten minutes of hard work, and hopefully a good five or six cycles of success, stop and do something your dog loves to do: give him a chew or a cuddle, or take him out for a walk. It needs to be a very positive experience as this will impact the way the dog's brain stores all the information you have taught him. Allow him to rest afterwards and give him something to chew and settle down. Keep an eye out for dreaming in sleep; as your dog enters the REM stage he may well be more active, processing all the new information he has learnt.

EXAMPLES AND TRAINING

Here are some simple examples of super-training for you to work up from. Some training is obvious; for example, if you are worried that if your dog gets out of the garden or is released off-lead he will not come back, then the 'come' command will be critically useful. You should start in an average enclosed space, possibly your back garden, depending on its size and security, and work on the 'come' command with super-training.

Recall
The first thing to do is show your dog that you have treats; the high value ones work

Super-training the recall should start in an area with few distractions. Ask your dog to sit and wait, just as Giles is displaying, while you move away.

The recall should be direct – notice how straight Giles is in returning at the call.

best for mental motivation, because your dog really wants that chicken! Then as the dog walks away call the command you want to use. It is normally a good idea to use something other than the dog's name as you might not want to super-train a name. For this example we will use 'come'; you might say the dog's name first then 'come', but not just the name. So we call softly 'Barney come' just once and wait for Barney to come back. Ideally – and this is where many people go wrong – you say it just once and, to begin with, when Barney is coming to you anyway because he doesn't know what you are asking of him yet. As soon as he gets within hand range, hold the treat out and as he takes it click the clicker once.

The simple solution now is to repeat this method over and over again and with most dogs this will be enough to train a dog to return when asked. But we are not just looking for a basic training method, we want to super-train the action so that you know that in almost any eventuality Barney will be coming back to you. So now that we have spent a week or so working in the back garden for no more than ten to fifteen minutes at a time, we can move on to make it harder although the principle is the same. A good example of making it harder might be to call him, 'Barney come' from one room to another so that he needs to pass from the kitchen to the lounge and then he gets the click and an immediate treat. We could add other people into the equation so that one or more people use the command, but you need to ensure that the process is identical to that which you use: a single command, the click and the treat all in perfect sequence. Then you could start to engage him with a toy but the process is the same: give him the toy or a chew, walk away, command, click, treat when he comes to you. From this point on you are adding distractions which would normally prevent Barney from listening to you, but you are making this one command an underlying requirement for everything he does and as such it should

When the recall command is super-trained your dog should come away from any stimuli you need him to, be it dog, person, horse or otherwise!

not be used as a negative either to him or a situation. He must continually see it as a benefit and his brain will override anything else to ensure that he achieves that benefit.

At this stage you can go out into public places, starting slowly to begin with. If he doesn't immediately return don't tell him off. This is still part of the learning process and any negativity when he comes back will teach him a bad association. As time moves on and you continue the conditioning it shouldn't matter if he is swimming in a lake, playing with his best friend or even if he spies the lovely-looking lady labrador next door, he will instantly return. At some point near the end of the first few weeks of training you can begin to offer more and more of the lower value treats but it's a good idea to sometimes use the high value to maintain interest as described earlier. Toys also make great rewards and remember that sniffer, tracker and even police dogs are regularly trained this way.

Something as simple as the come command can transform stressful walks in the park or countryside by making you more confident in your control of your dog. It can also be helpful with dogs who are fearful of strangers or other animals, and for dogs who are noisy when out or who defecate in unappreciated areas.

Watch Me

The 'watch me' command is a fantastic technique to train for three valuable reasons:

Toys that the dog can hold, such as this large ball, can be useful to direct the dog's mouthing energy away from threatening stimuli.

You can super-train the routine holding of items. This is particularly useful for dogs with potential concerns about threatening stimuli.

1. It encourages the dog to focus on you and away from possible concerns, but also teaches the dog to keep an eye on what you're doing. This is invaluable on and off the lead as it stops 'switching off', because they are taught to consistently 'check in' and follow you when required.
2. This focus not only improves obedience in all areas because of the increase in attention, but it can also prevent stress and concern building because the dog is focused on a calm source (you).
3. The 'watch me' is a brilliant tool for counter-conditioning as described throughout this book. When your dog makes eye contact with you and remains calm, stimuli can appear less threatening because you are taking control of the situation. By rewarding this attention focus and calm behaviour, you can teach a new emotional response to a threatening situation.

The 'watch me' works most effectively when it becomes automatic and super-trained, and dogs react instantly and voluntarily. These dogs watch their handlers as soon as they see a concerning stimulus and the handler can then act accordingly. It really is a fantastic way to enhance bonds and control between dogs and their owners while helping in desensitization and many other training methods. For example, if you know that bicycles worry your dog, then as soon as you see one approaching you give the 'watch me' command, and this redirects his attention from the bike onto you. Remember that when dogs are concerned by a stimulus it's in their best interest to focus intently on it and work out what's going on. If someone threatening you approached with a weapon, you would probably keep your eyes focused on the point of concern. This is precisely what your dog experiences and it gets worse the more he has learnt a negative association. The 'watch me' transfers this stress and with further reinforcement over time teaches a new way of behaving.

This command is very useful in the counter-conditioning process, which is a method whereby you substitute one particular behaviour for another. The dog learns the 'watch me' command most effectively when he is calm and relaxed because, as discussed, stress is an enemy to learning. Also dogs are more likely to associate the action with this state. In other words, in the case of the bicycles you are conditioning him to be calm and relaxed in the presence of cyclists. Eventually this state will replace the previous concern so that he will no longer feel the need to bark anxiously or defensively as a cyclist whizzes past.

How to Train the 'Watch Me'

- Start the training in a quiet location with few distractions. Your dog can be off- or on-lead depending on his level of attention. The garden is a great place to start as your dog knows where he is; it is contained and you can limit the distractions.
- While your dog is on the lead pick a moment when he is looking elsewhere to ask, 'watch me'. Use a friendly tone in a higher pitch than normal, and as he looks at you, reward (click and treat if trained up).
- Take a few paces forward and ask again. If he responds, reward once again.
- Before you take him out to another location, ensure he responds to the command when you are walking around the garden.

Giles is displaying a perfect 'watch me', making eye contact while moving.

- Progress to new locations but only those that are reasonably quiet. This is because a distracted, stressed or fearful dog has difficulty hearing you because his attention is totally focused on the point of concern.
- When asking, limit the command to one or two vocals on each occasion.

This will ensure that he remains responsive to the word. If he does not respond, it's likely that he is too excited by the environment to 'hear' you. Move on and ask again when you know he is less involved in what is going on around him. Slow the pace or stop to make things easier for him if he is finding it difficult to learn. As with all training, it should be carried out when you have the most chance of success.

- Aim to achieve the 'watch me' command while walking along, and even to get brief eye contact while still moving.

The 'watch me' can be a fantastic tool to take a dog's attention away from a possible fearful stimulus. This means that you can reward the calm behaviour and support the reinforcement of positive emotions around the source of concern, thus reducing or eliminating the concern.

With practice and super-training conditioning, the response to this command will become 'automatic'. Furthermore, in a situation that your dog finds stressful, he may even turn to 'watch' you when you have not asked him to; this would show that you had successfully modified your dog's reaction to anxiety-provoking stimuli.

WHAT ELSE TO TRAIN?

Larger dogs who pull on the lead will always benefit from sitting on command

Note my hand position in this photograph, with a treat inside to lure his head into the right position. Giles is looking to me for the next direction.

These two dogs are automatically waiting for their 'humans' to catch up out on a walk. The 'watch me' command can be an excellent way to enhance this.

Giles has settled comfortably with his weight over to one side and begins to remain stationary on command; the palm hand signal communicates what is desired.

for obvious reasons, not least because it means that you are not straining to hold them from walking into traffic when you are trying to cross the road. 'Stay' is possibly the hardest command to master and causes issues for most trainers in some way, shape or form, because normally your dog or puppy is a sociable creature and they want to be with you and make contact with you as often as possible. This is where super-training and mat training cross over and I have discussed that in detail already in this book. To super-train the stay command effectively you must

once again develop it gradually, and I have put together the following points to guide you in the process. A true, fast-responding sit is an invaluable tool to teach your dog in any posture.

- Start in a quiet location inside or outside.
- Ask your dog to target a particular area (possibly a mat) and sit, then lie down.
- Once in the down posture ask him to 'settle' and shift his weight over to the side so that he is comfortable.

Giles is remaining confidently still even though I am walking behind him in this photograph and am out of sight.

- Then ask 'stay' clearly, using a hand signal to help.
- For early training don't go anywhere and just wait for a few seconds before releasing him.
- Build this time until your dog can successfully remain still with you standing by his side.
- Now start taking steps back, one at a time, stopping and rewarding him for each successful event. If he gets it wrong just guide him back and start again; you may have to go back to an easier stage.
- As you advance, practise walking behind your dog, getting him used to you being out of sight.
- The final stage involves leaving your dog altogether (out of sight), but remember that this may take time to achieve. What is most important is that each stage is reinforced correctly so that your dog is practising the correct way to behave.

EXTRAS

So far I've discussed the particular commands to super-train that are most useful in behaviour modification. Teaching your dog new behaviours and tricks using super-training can, however, be a great way to mentally exercise your dog.

To decide what you should super-train comes down to what you need to get from your dog, but making walks less stressful and less dangerous is likely to mean that they will happen more often, resulting in a happier dog and a better relationship. A happy dog in the home, who is not shouted at and doesn't need to be locked away in a cage or separate room because of antisocial behaviour, is an obvious must-have and not a bonus. Additional skills to super-train include not going upstairs, staying off sofas, going to the toilet on command, barking or being silent, targeting a hand, mat or other item. This training should never be used as a punishment; the list can be as long or as short as you require. The aim is to have a happy, well-behaved and obedient dog who is a pleasure to live with.

Giles is performing a down to hand signals only; as you progress with your training you too can achieve this. His expression is intent, eager and responsive.

13 CONCLUSION

Problem dogs can be of any breed, sexual status, or age and belong to absolutely anyone. The interpretation of the severity of these concerns varies from person to person. There are, however, universal concerns with which owners struggle on a daily basis, and in worst case scenarios owners may even contemplate having to part with their dogs. The effect of problem behaviour on the people concerned ranges from mere irritation to distress, fear and even injury. Similarly, dogs affected are often equally distressed and depressed. My aim through this book has

Successfully tackling problem behaviour results in regaining harmony in your relationship. The other side effect is happiness for owner and dog alike, as this little dog's face sums up perfectly.

been to help you tackle these concerns directly with practical advice for everyday scenarios. I also wanted to help you understand the many factors that surround and influence behaviour and the vital part they have to play in treating the issues you are having.

To conclude this book I want to highlight one of the most essential pieces of advice I've tried to stress in every chapter. Successfully modifying behaviour problems requires changes to be made. These may be slight or major, but will make the difference between success or failure. Changes to one area or many, such as your dog's health, environment, experience, and the treatment he receives, can support actions and training intended to make a difference.

While it's vital to have rules and be consistent with your dog for successful cohabitation, I have tried to show you that you need not use brutality in order to change behaviour. In fact its use is detrimental for a wide variety of reasons. Successfully modifying problem behaviour can take days, weeks, months and sometimes years to achieve. I will leave you with the knowledge that through patience, understanding and determination you can help your dog overcome problem behaviour in a way that you once thought impossible.

FURTHER READING

Abrantes, R.A. (2005) *The Evolution of Canine Social Behaviour*, USA, Wakan Tanka Publishers

Aloff, A. (2005) *Canine Body Language: A Photographic Guide*, Dogwise, Wenatachee, USA

Coppinger, R. and A., (2004) *Dogs: A Startling New Understanding of Canine Origin, Behaviour and Evolution*, Crosskeys Select Books, London

Eatin, B. (2010) Dominance: *Fact or fiction?* Dogwise Publishing

Mech, D.L. (1999). 'Alpha status, dominance, and division of labor in wolf packs', *Canadian Journal of Zoology* 77: 1196-1203

Range, F., Horn, L., *et al.* (2009). 'The absence of reward induces inequity aversion in dogs' in *Proceedings of the National Academy of Sciences* 106 (1): 340-345.

Rugaas, T. (2006), *On Talking Terms with Dogs: Calming Signals*, Dogwise Publishing

Topál, J., Miklósi, A., *et al.* (1998). 'Attachment Behavior in Dogs (*Canis familiaris*): A New Application of Ainsworth's (1969) Strange Situation Test' in the *Journal of Comparative Psychology* 112(3): 219-229.

Serpell, J. (1995). *The Domestic Dog: Its Evolution, Behaviour and Interactions with People*, Cambridge University Press

Trut, L.N., Plyusnina, I.Z., et al. (2004) 'An Experiment on Fox Domestication and Debatable Issues of Evolution of the Dog Journal' in *Russian Journal of Genetics* 40(6): 644-655.

Vidovi, V.V., Šteti, V.V., et al. (1999). 'Pet Ownership, Type of Pet and Socio-Emotional Development of School Children' in Anthrozoos: *A Multidisciplinary Journal of The Interactions of People & Animals* 12(4): 211-217 Wilson, C.C. and Turner, D.C., eds. (1997), SAGE Publications Inc.

FURTHER INFORMATION

www.apbc.org.uk/
The Association of Pet Animal Behaviour Councillors is an international network of qualified pet behaviour counsellors who work on referral from vets to treat behaviour problems in dogs and other pets.

www.asab.nottingham.ac.uk/index.php
The Association for Study of Animal Behaviour was founded in 1936 to promote the study of animal behaviour. Membership is open to all who share this interest and the association lists their certified behaviourists.

www.battersea.org.uk/dogs
Battersea re-homes dogs all over the country, provided that you are able to collect the dog from one of their three sites: Battersea London, Battersea Old Windsor and Battersea Brands Hatch.

www.bluecross.org.uk
The Blue Cross has eleven re-homing centres around the country. They promote responsible ownership and practical care of the animals they hope to re home.

www.dogpages.org.uk
Dogpages is a non-commercial site run solely by volunteers. The aim of the site is to offer helpful advice and information across a wide breadth of dog-related subjects.

www.dogstrust.org.uk
The Dogs Trust is the largest canine welfare charity in the UK and has seventeen centres around the country including Northern Ireland. They re-home thousands of dogs a year and provide owners with help at each stage of the re-homing process.

www.thekennelclub.org.uk
The primary objective of the Kennel Club is to 'promote in every way, the general improvement of dogs'. The Kennel Club was founded in 1873 and is able to offer dog owners an in-depth source of information, experience and advice on dog welfare, dog health, dog training and dog breeding.

INDEX